M000200202

THE ART OF RETREATS

THE ART
of RETREATS

A LEADER'S JOURNEY
TOWARD CLARITY,
BALANCE, *and* PURPOSE

FABRICE
DESMARESCAUX

LIONCREST
PUBLISHING

THE ART OF RETREATS
A Leader's Journey Toward Clarity, Balance, and Purpose

ISBN   978-1-5445-2638-6   *Hardcover*
        978-1-5445-2636-2   *Paperback*
        978-1-5445-2637-9   *Ebook*

Illustrations by Jocelyne Lee Dubos

To my parents, Jean and Liliane
To my wife, Shan, and my daughter, Celia
And to all my past, present, and future teachers

CONTENTS

INTRODUCTION

As you begin this book, you may have a few presuppositions. You may believe, for example, that retreats are reserved for celebrities, hippies, or the lucky few who do not have responsibilities in *real* life. Living a contemplative life is the special privilege of spiritual seekers, right?

Or perhaps you believe leaders should focus on what they do best: running organizations. They should leave the reflecting to others. After all, leaders are not intellectuals or contemplatives but people driven to action and success.

In this book, I invite you to question these presuppositions. Along the way, I will show you that the opposite is often true: Leaders achieve greater clarity, balance, and purpose when they combine "acting" with "being" and take time to retreat. And the higher they go, the greater the rewards for marrying "action" and "contemplation."

Let me explain.

If you're reading this, chances are that you are in a leadership position or aspiring to be in one. You work hard to take care of business, earn money, and satisfy your bosses, clients, investors, and staff. You may have a family and be raising children. With whatever time is left in your day after that, you sleep or exercise or get involved with your community.

But even if you feel you have everything under control in the outer world, how do you care for your inner world? And how do you ensure that your true self is not at odds with your external persona?

These questions have been at the heart of my life for the last twenty years. Earlier in my career, I was a business executive and a partner at a prestigious consulting firm, but I was interested in spirituality, psychology, and human development before ever entering the business world. Once I began progressing in leadership roles, I struggled to reconcile my longing for authenticity and purpose with the demands of business. Eventually, it dawned on me: this is not an either-or dilemma. We can integrate both worlds, if we only decide to walk through certain gateways. In the last decade or so, I have guided senior business leaders on that path. Today, I work as a coach, retreat leader, and leadership advisor to businesses of all sizes. I love supporting my clients in this quest to find clarity, balance, and purpose in their personal and professional lives.

The leaders I work with know how to play the leadership game. They are efficient, driven, and focused. They have significant responsibilities and influence, and they deliver results to their stakeholders. They excel at what I call growth in the horizontal dimension—the material world.

But there is another dimension, the vertical one, that allows us to deepen our leadership. Depth is not about efficiency, scale, or shareholder value. Instead, it is about connecting with the things that give us meaning: self-awareness, presence, meaningful relationships based on caring, equanimity and compassion, embracing the complexity of the world with curiosity, life and death, wisdom, and ultimately, purpose.

My clients would love to spend more time looking within, but they have neither the time nor the method to do so. The demands on their time are such that they feel fragmented and scattered. Targets are increasingly ambitious. The combination of globalization, changing demographics, global warming, new technologies, big data, artificial intelligence, a pandemic, and the reality of inequalities surfacing in every field has created a complexity never seen before. Today, leaders reach a milestone, and several new priorities emerge instantly. There is no end in sight. It is never good enough.

To succeed in this relentless environment, one must excel at the horizontal dimension. This means exacerbating character traits such as ambition and drive and focusing on winning to the extent that other parts of life—like relationships, physical and mental health, or spirituality—are neglected. Somewhere in the process of fitting into the business culture and reaching for the top, leaders often become lopsided; their brightest qualities, such as passion, serenity, equanimity, generosity, and compassion, are eclipsed. They lose touch with the vertical dimension.

I wrote this book after spending countless hours with leaders who are all confronting the same questions I did. They want to achieve leadership depth. They've mastered the horizontal dimension but struggle to explore the vertical one. What can they do to look inside and regain wholeness? How can they find clarity and balance amidst this ever-increasing complexity? How do they reconnect with what makes them truly human? And how do they ensure that they ultimately make a positive difference?

MY JOURNEY WITHIN

Spiritual traditions invite us to explore the depth of the vertical dimension. In my early thirties, full of naïve inspiration, I started a sitting practice to look within. This was a complete flop. Sitting in silence was like venturing into a deep cave without a lantern. My first reaction was to run back to the safety of the outside world. I hated the dark and the silence, which I promptly covered up with music. I hated the solitude and preferred to seek company. I concluded that meditation was a colossal waste of time. Like a hungry ghost, I resumed filling my inner emptiness with outer stimulation.

It was many years later, with greater maturity, that I finally accepted the darkness, and my eyes started discerning shapes and contours. In silence, I finally made out the faint messages of my inner voices. And in solitude, I realized that I was never alone.

Nothing destined me to seek a contemplative path. I grew up in the horizontal world of action. In my thirties, as a partner with the consulting firm McKinsey & Company, I advised leaders and boards of banks and insurance companies. I later joined one of these banks and oversaw a business with a few thousand staff, five hundred branches, and revenue in the hundreds of millions of dollars.

My perspective shifted when, in my forties, I dedicated myself to the executive search profession. I became a "headhunter," recruiting senior executives and building top teams for financial institutions. I measured how, despite their rich compensation packages and unbridled career ambitions, many of these leaders were suffering from a lack of inner guidance.

I explored with my clients what would make them and their teams more fulfilled and purposeful, without sacrificing the short-term imperatives of profits and growth. As a discreet behind-the-scenes advisor, I asked my clients: is this an either-or situation? Do you have to sacrifice your inner self to achieve career success? Can a leadership team align on goals that both satisfy their stakeholders and their desire to have a positive impact on the world?

Because I was raised in the West but lived most of my adult life in Asia, I blend Eastern and Western traditions into my work and invite leaders into a journey that is pragmatic and rational while also inviting awe and inspiration. I will invite you into that same journey throughout this book.

THE PATH BEFORE YOU

Far from being dogmatic, this book offers a realistic path to balance our need for action with an increased longing for reflection, meaning, and purpose.

Together, we will explore four millennia of human wisdom—not in a theoretical way but interactively, through discussions and practical exercises. All you need for this journey is curiosity and the desire to achieve greater leadership clarity, balance, and purpose.

Along the way, you will need to carve out some time for yourself, and I will show you how. This may sound counterintuitive; time is already so scarce! For now, you will simply have to trust the process. As you do, you will see why personal retreats have been the secret weapon of great leaders since the dawn of humanity. Leaders who retreat regularly radiate presence, clarity, inspiration, purpose, creativity, and wisdom. If you accompany me on this journey, you, too, will discover how to access your inner resources, those you instinctively know you have but struggle to access amid everyday distractions.

You have an opportunity to rediscover the path that many other greats have trodden before you. There is no miracle cure, and I am no magician. The road that I am inviting you to walk with me has been explored for millennia by spiritual sages, philosophers, mystics, artists, psychologists, and neuroscientists. What makes our journey unique is that we will approach it from the perspective of a leader facing the challenges of the modern business world.

WHAT TO EXPECT

In the first part of the book, I review the challenges that leaders face and how personal retreats can be a marvelous leadership tool. I will show you how to structure a retreat, whether it lasts two hours or two weeks. And I will share tips on overcoming the initial resistance to taking time for yourself.

In the second part of the book, we will explore contemplative themes that are critical to deepening leadership. Most are counterintuitive and will challenge the unbalanced ideology of busyness, superficiality, power, and accumulation. To guide you, I will offer simple reflections, or contemplations, that will allow you to explore and deepen your own leadership style.

Many of these reflections are inspired by my work with other leaders—people who have valiantly walked this path with me. It has been a privilege to share their journeys. To protect confidentiality, names and details have been altered.

The path that I have charted for you is inspired by a quest to marry doing and being, action and contemplation, horizontality and verticality.

Let's walk this path together!

PART I

THE ART
of RETREATS

Chapter 1

THE CHALLENGE
of LEADERSHIP

"I WANT TO FEEL ALIVE AGAIN!" SERGIO TOLD ME AT THE beginning of our work together.

Nothing about Sergio suggested he lacked vitality. An imposing figure, he carried himself with authority and confidence. Sergio had been chief executive officer of a regional airline until he retired in his early fifties. Despite his personal investment activities and board seats, Sergio felt lost and useless.

"I used to wake up full of energy in the morning. I loved going to work. Today, I'm not sure what I should be doing anymore." To fill the void inside, Sergio had accepted too many appointments. His days were busy, but hyperactivity was no longer enough to distract Sergio from a deeper questioning. His sense of self-worth was tied to the title on his business card, and since he was no longer at the top of a large organization, he no longer felt worthy.

I decided to initiate Sergio into the art of retreats. Rather than encouraging him to look for more prestigious appointments, I challenged him to do nothing for a while. We took baby steps at first. No point going cold turkey for someone who has worked twelve-hour days all his life. "Just disconnect your phone for a couple of hours and go for a walk in the woods," I suggested. "Try that three times a week, early in the morning, instead of watching the news."

After a couple of weeks, Sergio became accustomed to spending time without checking messages. I invited him to write about the thoughts and emotions that came up during his time alone.

Progressively, we continued expanding the time that Sergio spent in silence, solitude, and nature. In parallel, we reflected together on what gave him satisfaction in life. After three months, he was ready for more. He flew to Italy, where he owned a house on the seaside. There, he enjoyed nice food, walks in the sunset, and a few games of golf. The time alone allowed him to deepen his reflections.

Sergio came back from this retreat energized and inspired. He stepped down from several boards that did not satisfy his sense of purpose. He severed his ties with a business partner who was causing him more anxiety than joy and dedicated himself to the chairmanship of a logistics company where he felt he could play an impactful role in mentoring the young and ambitious CEO.

Sergio's experience is not unique among leaders. When I first started working with him, he was resistant to the idea of retreats. You may have your own reservations. That's only natural. Still, I will invite you into this journey because I know that you, like Sergio, can experience greater clarity, balance, and purpose through taking a step outside of your "normal."

THE PRICE OF SUCCESS

I get it. You are a busy leader. Work and personal commitments keep you engaged from the moment you wake up until the time you go to sleep. Whether you're the CEO of a global corporation, a senior executive, or a small business owner, you are responsible for creating an inspiring vision and directing or influencing others.

You are successful and proud of what you have already accomplished. You may be under pressure, dealing with complexity and striving to achieve ever-increasing objectives. No decision you make is ever obvious. If it were, others would already have made it. That's why you are the leader in the first place.

You can never completely relax. You want to stay connected, and consciously or unconsciously, you check your phone a hundred times a day. You go on vacations, but by the time you unwind and settle down, it's already time to get back.

Every now and then, a small voice tells you everything is not as perfect as it looks. But because you're always on the move, you rarely have time to take stock of your life and ask the important questions: Am I on the right track? Am I living up to my potential? Is this what I am meant to be? You would love to address these fundamental questions, but the introspection will have to wait until you are less busy. There's only one problem: it doesn't seem like things will ever slow down.

This story—Sergio's story—is shared by many leaders. It is also my story.

I grew up in Paris and trained as a mathematician and a civil engineer. I later earned a business degree from INSEAD and obtained a job in strategy consulting. My education and career left little room for contemplation. With two master's degrees in my pocket, I believed mostly in science, free markets, meritocracy, and minimal government intervention. As you can imagine, France was not my ideal playground, so I left at the age of twenty-four and worked in London and Madrid before settling down between Singapore and Jakarta in my early thirties.

I went on to enjoy a long stretch in consulting, which culminated at McKinsey & Company. Four years in, I ended up leading our financial services practice in Southeast Asia. When I left "The Firm," as we called it, I joined a bank to oversee its consumer banking division. Life was good, with all the perks of the senior executive lifestyle: business class travel around the world, luxury hotels, car and driver, and a fat stock option package.

But outer success can never compensate for a lack of purpose. I had just turned forty and was recently separated. I found my work meaningless. Maybe I was just having a midlife crisis, but there was no time for introspection. I was constantly on air-planes, working long hours, and had no one and no tools to help me think clearly about what I really wanted to do. I was at a complete loss.

It had never occurred to me to change careers. McKinsey and banking were my life, and for many years, I had aspired to reach the top and become a bank CEO. It was only when I finally took time to reflect, on a retreat in Bali, that I first had a glimpse of my true calling: supporting executives on topics of leadership and personal growth. The shift happened gradually, through trial and error and a lot of angst. I became more aware of what activities energized me, and which ones drained me. Eventually, the path became clearer. My purpose was not to develop strategies and restructuring plans; it was to build leadership teams and develop individual leaders.

I wish I'd had the guidance to figure out this life transition earlier. I know today that my situation was in no way unique, and that all leaders face similar challenges:

- Our time is fragmented, as we try to squeeze more and more activities into the same twenty-four hours. We are always connected and reachable. Periods of uninterrupted thinking become rarer and shorter.

- We are under increasing pressure to deliver results that are always more ambitious. Our bosses, shareholders, and clients are more demanding and set the bar higher every year. We feel that we are only as good as our last success, and we need to prove ourselves over and over again.

- We operate in a context that is increasingly complex. It is harder to see the big picture in an interconnected world. Whatever we do here may provoke an unexpected reaction there. It is harder to see the connection between cause and effect.

All these factors often prevent us from having the necessary breathing space to elevate ourselves and, with discernment, shape how we should lead ourselves and others.

Let's examine these challenges in more detail.

FRAGMENTATION

Fragmentation shows up in our relationship with time. It seems like there just aren't enough hours in the day, and we feel starved for time. We react to this famine by shortening our interactions with others for the sake of efficiency. For example, "I'd love to talk to you about this, but I really need to answer this client email now," says Vanessa to a young associate who comes to her with a question. "Let's take this offline," cuts Salman during a staff meeting, when one of his vice presidents raises an objection to a new investment. They both know offline means never.

When we feel that crucial questions are not explored in depth, or that meaningful conversations are cut short because we need to run to another meeting, we're suffering from time famine.

Fragmentation is also caused by interruptions, and our devices are often the culprits. Consciously or not, we let our gadgets intrude, or "notify" us rudely hundreds of times a day. Our phones light up or chime incessantly, interrupting our concentration and drawing our attention like a red cloak attracts the bull. We check an incoming message, and our attention is caught by another email, which reminds us that we need to ask a supplier to send his proposal. It could be twenty minutes before we realize that we have been lured off track. Ultimately, our lives become a series of "time confetti," to use the term coined by journalist Brigid Schulte.

Despite abundant scientific evidence that shows our brains are wired to handle one activity at a time, we believe we can multitask. We try to focus, but we are fighting against apps designed by distraction experts. Whether checking email messages, Facebook posts, or YouTube videos, our brains are hijacked by corporations that make billions selling our eyeballs to advertisers. It is a losing battle, as Tristan Harris illustrated in his documentary *The Social Dilemma*.

Writer Linda Stone calls the act of performing simultaneous activities that demand cognitive alertness "continuous partial attention." Talking on the phone while driving, writing an email during a conference call, carrying a conversation at dinner while texting under the table. Sound familiar?

When you practice continuous partial attention, Stone suggests, you're diverting attention from your primary task and constantly scanning for people, activities, or opportunities that seem, in this instant, more important. You're always in high alert. This leads to increased stress and an inability to concentrate on the present moment. It hampers your reflection, contemplation, and thoughtful decision-making. The constant connectedness also affects relationships, lowers productivity levels, and leads to overstimulation and a lack of fulfillment.

More deeply, you feel fragmented when your mind, heart, and body are misaligned, or when you are pulled in different directions by conflicting priorities. Nicolas, a financial adviser for the ultrawealthy, is torn between his desire to live close to nature and his professional need to be located near a financial center. According to Nicolas, "My wife and I would love a simpler life in the countryside. But I need to meet my clients regularly and can't afford to commute back and forth. Zoom just doesn't allow me to build true relationships." Nicolas also feels fragmented when he considers his professional and lifestyle choices. He loves advising Asian entrepreneurs and wealthy families. But to keep up appearances, he must maintain an expensive lifestyle, including vacations in luxury resorts and private schools for his kids. Nicolas remarked, "Deep inside, a voice tells me that it is time for a new phase in my life. I have ignored this voice until now, but it won't shut up."

Fragmentation keeps us awake at night, and we mourn the days when everything seemed to be falling in place perfectly. When mind, body, and heart are not working in unison, we lose integrity.

PRESSURE

In a global economy, our competitors could be in our backyard or twelve time zones away. The winners dominate the world and receive rewards of unprecedented proportions. In this winner-takes-all configuration, the pressure to succeed is enormous.

Like cancer cells, businesses can't stop, and won't stop, expanding. Leaders seek exponential growth to satisfy their investors. No CEO can ever say, "We have a satisfying business, and we'll aim for the same revenue as we did last year." Growth is mandatory. Terrified that a competitor will disrupt their businesses, leaders relentlessly attempt to stay ahead. Call it creative destruction or paranoia, but the message is clear: enjoying today what you created yesterday is a recipe for losers. There is no place to rest and call home. Chronic fear and stress, not serenity, is the natural state of executives caught in that game.

The pressure to grow is compounded by the stress of adapting to new technologies. Technology promised to make our lives better by automating the least rewarding tasks. But for the last fifty years, productivity gains have not been passed to the executives. For them, there's no shorter workweek or increased leisure time.

The beneficiaries are the corporations and their shareholders. Sure, leaders might drive better cars and have an infinite choice of numbing online entertainment. But they pay for their consumerist comfort with their time. Executives today work, on average, ten hours more per week than those of the previous generation.

Technology does come with benefits. It allows us to work from anywhere in the world. This was certainly useful during the COVID pandemic. On the flip side, we can now connect with colleagues day and night. It's no wonder that sleep deprivation is frequent among global executives. It's always 10:00 a.m. somewhere.

Heidegger, the German philosopher, warned us about the risk of losing our human identity and fusing with technology. We expect technology to be the solution to all our suffering, by automating our jobs and our decisions and offering us endless distraction in return. Today, we should ask ourselves: are we the masters of our technology, or have we become its servants?

COMPLEXITY

Our business systems are complex and interconnected. It is now difficult to connect actions with results. Often, despite the advice of experts, outcomes are far from what we anticipated. We can launch a probe to Mars, but we can't foresee the effects of a pandemic on our business.

In some ways, complexity is not a new challenge for leaders. Julius Caesar paved the way for the Roman empire. The Tang dynasty built a world-class civil service system. Thomas Watson Sr. turned IBM into a powerhouse. Could they grasp all the implications of their decisions? I doubt it.

But the level of complexity that leaders face today is unprecedented. Their employees are better educated and better informed. Every decade, a new wave of technologies revolutionizes how we deliver our services. And many businesses have expanded to a global scale.

We expect leaders to predict the unpredictable. Strategic plans and budgets intend to make us feel like we are in control. In reality, we know deep inside that we are no more in control than a boat captain who has lost his sails and rudder. We face a storm with a pair of oars.

Who can claim they understand global supply chains, financial systems, or the internet? Who masters the intricacies of motivating a workforce? Who knows how to transform a corporate culture or control a pandemic? Even governments and large corporations have little idea of the connection between causes and effects.

Complexity is the greatest challenge for leaders today. As complexity increases, we realize that our deterministic and predictive tools are imperfect. Small perturbations create big changes, and we have no idea why. Maybe our fancy tools help us explain what happened after the fact, but that's not so helpful when we're in the midst of the fog.

THE IDEOLOGY OF BUSYNESS

Most leaders attempt to respond quantitatively to fragmentation, pressure, and complexity. They work harder and faster. They assume that longer hours will help solve the challenges they face.

This thinking stems from the industrial revolution, when outputs were proportional to inputs. If I lengthen the workers' hours by 20 percent, I also increase their production by 20 percent, right? Not quite. What worked in an industrial setting does not apply to twenty-first century leaders. But we still operate by that paradigm. In our minds, busier is better.

The ideology of busyness is pervasive. We love to describe ourselves as busy. We pack our schedules, and there are not enough hours in the day. Even on vacation, we check emails, take "important" calls, and work on deals. Empty spaces in our calendars, especially for silence or solitude, scare us. We look at them with guilt or anguish.

Technology and communication devices are key culprits. Heidegger warned us in 1954. In a book titled *The Question Concerning Technology*, he wrote: "Everywhere we remain unfree and chained to technology, whether we passionately affirm or deny it. But we are delivered over to it in the worst possible way when we regard it as something neutral; for this conception of it, to which today we particularly like to do homage, makes us utterly blind to the essence of technology."

We may be victims, but we are willing victims. To the question, "How are you?", a fashionable answer is, "Busy!" We say this in a complaining tone, as if we have no choice and are the compliant drone to an abusive taskmaster. James Flaherty, a pioneer in the field of coaching, observed in his *Integral Coaching* course: "The possibility of work and communication gets translated into an obligation to do it."

Our vocabulary reveals our impotence to control our time. For example, "I would love to have dinner with you, but I must finish this report" or "I would love to play tennis next week, but this is our budget period."

We now work at an accelerated pace, and the world's digital clock seems to be on overdrive. Time has become the yardstick by which we measure our effectiveness. We must make decisions fast, and we see time spent thinking and analyzing as a weakness more than a strength. Fast is synonymous with good.

When we are not busy and fast, we feel deficient. Everyone else seems to have an important mission, and we don't. But take a closer look, and you will realize that busyness is more an ideology than a necessity. As researchers Belleza, Paharia, and Keinan have pointed out in a paper titled *Conspicuous Consumption of Time*, busyness, an overworked lifestyle, and lack of leisure time have become a status symbol, particularly in the United States.

What's clear is that busyness cannot be the solution to your challenges. Your work as a leader, after all, is not measured in hours. You cannot achieve clarity of thinking, balance, and purpose by working an extra 20 percent. You may numb yourself by staying hyperactive. But the question "What are you pursuing exactly?" will always come back to you at night when you lay awake in the dark. You need a different solution.

FACING THE CONSEQUENCES

Busyness has a huge cost. We lose the qualities that make us successful: clear thinking, balance, and a sense of purpose.

Long work hours, business travel, multitasking, jetlag, and stress decrease our cognitive abilities. Busyness distracts us from our innate ability for clear thinking and calm.

An agitated mind cannot understand markets, competitors, technological and societal shifts, regulations, geopolitics, and environmental issues. It succumbs to cognitive biases and makes poor decisions.

When you're constantly on the go, your health and relationships suffer. You channel your extraordinary discipline and drive into work. You neglect exercise, nutrition, sleep, and quality time with loved ones. The very qualities that made you successful are now turning against you. You overlook your physical, emotional, and mental health. It's no wonder many senior executives suffer from anxiety, attention deficit disorder, and anger, while others fall into depression or addiction to drugs, alcohol, and sex.

Former Harvard Business School professor Clay Christensen once said, "The pursuit of success leads us to allocating every ounce of energy, instinctively and unconsciously, to whatever activities give us the most immediate evidence of achievement. Our careers provide that immediate evidence of achievement: we close a sale, we ship a product, we finish a presentation, we close a deal, we get promoted, we get paid."

In contrast, as Christensen points out, investments in ourselves or our families don't pay off for a very long time.

When we make trade-offs in favor of short-term gains, we disconnect from our sense of purpose. Very few leaders are clear about their ultimate purpose. When I ask my clients about this, I often receive well-intentioned but shallow answers: "I love what I do" or "I love the lifestyle that comes with the job" or "I want to make an impact on people." Maybe you've said similar statements. There is nothing wrong with working for money, status, or power. But even if you get satisfaction from these external markers of success, you still need to connect with your deeper aspirations. It's still worth figuring out what life expects from you and not only what you expect from life.

IN SEARCH OF CLARITY, BALANCE, AND PURPOSE

Many leaders I work with are masters of the horizontal game. They've reached the top of the pyramid. But they still face fragmentation, pressure, and complexity. They long for greater depth. They aspire to achieve greater clarity, balance, and purpose. The stakes are enormous. These leaders not only influence many lives but also shape our collective future.

But where can leaders turn? How can they move beyond the ideology of busyness and find the answers they need?

Remember Sergio? Over the course of six months, he took regular short retreats. He spent time in his country house and with family in the United States. He sailed a boat in the Caribbean. Time alone, which seemed so frightening at first, became an enjoyable resource. With greater peace came discernment. Sergio resigned from several boards and focused his energy on the chairmanship of a logistics business. He designed an ambitious growth and acquisition strategy, which ultimately led to the takeover of a large competitor.

With greater control of his time, Sergio also found space to care for himself and exercise. He lost more than 40 pounds and regained the energy and fitness levels he had in his twenties. In his own words, he now felt alive again. He had found a way to clarity, balance, and purpose.

We have examined the major challenges facing modern executives. The following chapters capture my experience working with leaders like Sergio. Remember, there is no miracle cure. There is no instant leadership enlightenment. Instead, this book is an invitation to reflect together on these challenges and move forward step by step along a different path.

The next chapter will focus on the vertical dimension of leadership and the benefits of retreats. Let's continue exploring together!

Ten Signs You Need a Retreat

1. You find it difficult, at work or at home, to concentrate without interruption for more than one hour.
2. You can't spend a day without your phone, tablet, or computer.
3. You check emails and messages during meetings, and you may interrupt a conversation when you hear the chime of an incoming message.
4. Your board, shareholders, or boss asks you to deliver more every year.
5. You take vacations but find it difficult to disconnect from work and enjoy peace.
6. You sometimes wish for a simpler life.
7. You have not taken a long walk in nature in the last twelve months.
8. You keep restructuring your organization every few years.
9. The business problems you are asked to solve seem to have no solution.
10. Your business is unpredictable, and it is hard to determine precisely what factors drive success.

Additional Reflections

- How many of these signs were present at the beginning of your career?
- How many of these signs did your parents or grandparents exhibit?

Practice: Three Deep Breaths to Get Centered

The breath occupies a central place in contemplative practices. It is easy to notice, it is not associated with any religion, and it is always available. It requires no equipment and no app.

Breath is a source of life. With every inhalation, you absorb energy. With every outbreath, you let go of tension. When you take a deep breath from the belly, you engage your whole body in a rhythmic pattern. When you place your awareness on the breath, you effortlessly connect mind and body.

As a leader, you likely run from one meeting to the next. You line up videocalls back-to-back. You may not have time to pause and gather your thoughts. The simple practice of three deep breaths can help you make a conscious transition between meetings. These are a few precious moments to let go of the previous activity to be present for the next one.

For this practice, sit comfortably on a chair with your feet flat on the ground, not leaning back but sitting upright. Imagine that a thread, attached to the crown of your head, pulls toward the sky and lengthens your spine. Inhale through the nose. Let out a long exhale through the mouth.

Take three deep breaths, allowing the spine to lift as you inhale and the body to relax as you exhale. Then, let your breathing return to its natural pace.

Visualize reaching a place of calm and stillness. Your body is like a mountain, your breath like the wind, and your mind like the sky.

Feel gratitude for having this moment away from the noise and agitation of the world.

Chapter 2

THE ESSENCE *of* CONTEMPLATIVE LEADERSHIP

"YOU WANT ME TO DO WHAT?" SUSAN LOOKED AT ME in disbelief.

Here was a finance executive in her early fifties, ready to create a more purposeful life. Only she didn't think she'd have to go to the desert to find it.

The first time I met with Susan, we discussed her career, her relationships, her fears, and her aspirations. The picture of her life began to crystallize. Susan was responsible for finance at a large trading company headquartered in Dubai. A worldly executive, she had lived and worked on three continents. Her bosses thought of her as hardworking and competent. She loved her job and had a great relationship with her CEO, whom she had followed for many years. She and her husband were both in good health. So what more could she want?

Susan went on to share how she sometimes felt an existential void. Should she accept a job transfer to Canada? Should she retire? At times, she longed for a simpler life, away from the pressure of the corporate world. Perhaps she could move to Costa Rica and run a bed and breakfast?

I wasn't convinced. I knew that Susan was open to a change. But I also felt that her ideas were reactionary. She was prone to impulsive decisions: ten years ago, she had quit her job and moved to Thailand with her husband. After riding around the country on a motorcycle, they got bored. They returned to England six months later. Yet, she was looking for the next experience.

She knew her impulsivity was not always her best ally. But she couldn't identify what would energize her in her professional and personal life. She only knew *something* was missing.

I asked Susan to tune in to her inner wisdom. She was intelligent, articulate, and conscientious. She had the resources in her to discover her own solution. I encouraged her to listen to her soul. Susan was not a religious person, and I did not use "soul" in a spiritual sense. Instead, I explained that we must sometimes let the answers appear by themselves and not force them out with logic and reason.

Eventually, I asked Susan to start taking mini retreats. During these short breaks of a couple of hours, she sat by herself with a notebook. I wanted her to get in touch with herself without interruptions. Though she was hesitant at first, she came to love these segments of "me-time" and was able to learn much about her own desires and fears. After a few weeks of working with her, I suggested the big experiment: "Go spend a night alone in the desert. See what comes up." Again, she hesitated, but she took me up on the suggestion. Her time in the desert ultimately provided her the clarity she needed to take her next steps.

ACTION VS. CONTEMPLATION

Writing a book on retreats and contemplative leadership isn't easy. After all, "leadership" and "contemplation" are rarely found in the same sentence.

Leaders are people of action. They personify Doing. As leaders, we act in the world, most often in the pursuit of an explicit goal, monetary and short-term. We create grand visions, and we track progress with key performance indicators. We live in the horizontal dimension, the one that leads to greater worldly success.

As leaders, we are also suspicious of contemplatives. When someone suggests we should slow down and take a moment to look inside, we may agree it's a good idea. But there is usually something "more important" to do at that time.

As spiritual teacher Janet Drey wrote in her paper titled *Contemplative Leadership in Organizations*, "Who has time for introspection when I am barely keeping my head above water?"

Contemplatives exemplify Being. They live in a world that, at least to an outsider, appears still and silent. They spend time in solitude. They live in inspiring places like monasteries, cloisters, and ashrams. They listen to the call of the soul. No worries about profits and market share for contemplative types. Only the quest to become more acquainted with the soul. This is the vertical dimension that leads to greater presence, wisdom, and purpose.

Of course, connecting with the soul cannot happen in a noisy world. In *Let Your Life Speak*, Quaker educator Parker Palmer wrote:

> The soul is like a wild animal—tough, resilient, savvy, self-sufficient, and yet exceedingly shy. If we want to see a wild animal, the last thing we should do is to go crashing through the woods, shouting for the creature to come out. But if we are willing to walk quietly into the woods and sit silently for an hour or two at the base of a tree, the creature we are waiting for may well emerge, and out of the corner of an eye, we will catch a glimpse of the precious wildness we seek.

Herein lies the impossible contradiction. Leadership is about acting and doing. Contemplation is about letting go. Can we or should we reconcile the two? My answer is, of course, yes!

Leadership is a vocation, not a job. To respond to that calling, leaders must bring the quality of presence to their action. Being without Doing doesn't trigger change. But Doing without Being often leads to senseless action that will leave you feeling unfulfilled.

Action and contemplation are complementary, not incompatible. The two disciplines enrich and balance each other. Contemplation puts our leadership in perspective. It allows us to see a much more vibrant picture, rich in contrasts and colors.

THE RISK OF LOSING ONESELF

In our world full of pressure, fragmentation, and complexity, we risk losing ourselves. Most leaders are well-intentioned and responsible individuals. They believe in treating everyone with respect. They want to be good citizens in their communities. They use their leverage to multiply their impact and serve their constituents. Very few leaders wake up in the morning set to destroy the planet and its inhabitants for the sake of getting richer.

Yet, organizations, corporations, and governments regularly engage in reckless behaviors that go unchecked. The list of these actions is endless and includes:

- Production of traditional, nuclear, and biological weapons.
- Money laundering and corruption of domestic or foreign officials.
- Use of private data by tech companies for marketing use.
- Employment of children and forced labor in production chains and construction.

- Unfair treatment of contractors who end up working below minimum wage without medical coverage or benefits.
- Concentration of profits in low-tax havens.
- Recruitment and employment discrimination.
- Development of artificial intelligence that will lead to mass unemployment.
- Use of antibiotics in the food chain so that humans may soon become antibiotic resistant.
- Use of pesticides in the food chain that lead to large-scale destruction of ecosystems.
- Manufacturing and marketing unhealthy products such as cigarettes, soft drinks, and snacks, which may lead to obesity, cancers, diabetes, and cardiovascular disease.
- Inhuman treatment of animals in industrial farms, slaughterhouses, and laboratories.
- Deforestation, illegal logging, and unsustainable farming.
- Dumping of chemicals and animal waste in rivers and water table.
- Production of plastics for packaging that end up in the oceans.
- Manufacturing consumer goods, electronics, cars, and white goods without adequate recycling plans.
- Excessive use of single-use packaging.
- Unchecked carbon emissions or flouting regulations on emissions.
- Flouting regulations on financial services.

If most leaders have the best intentions, what's the disconnect? Why do these actions continue, and even multiply?

Unfortunately, organizations put leaders under tremendous pressure to perform. In turn, leaders worry that if they are the only ethical ones, they will lose out to their competitors. Many convince themselves over time that they are not accountable for the long-term impact of their decisions. After all, they won't be here anymore when the bill comes. The short-term must be the prime focus.

It's no wonder critical issues like global warming or environmental destruction are so difficult to address. Leaders have so few incentives to collaborate, adopt a long view, and behave in an ethical manner, and so many reasons to ignore the issues. And at the end of the day, they are only human.

THE RESPONSIBILITY OF LEADERSHIP

To rise above the noise, you must return to the initial call of leadership. Your vocation to lead comes with the responsibility to bring positive change to the world. The scale of your job doesn't matter. You may be a CEO, an entrepreneur, an advisor, or still early in your career. The moment you choose to lead others, you have acknowledged your agency and must act accordingly.

We are at a turning point in the history of mankind. On the one hand, as a species we live better, longer, and safer lives than ever before. We have benefited from science and modern liberal ideology. The previous centuries saw dramatic poverty, endless wars, and famines. Communism and fascism caused tens of millions of deaths. Liberalism, with its focus on human rights, civil liberties, democracy, and free enterprise, has brought us lasting peace, wealth, and health.

Yet, our liberal model is facing unprecedented challenges. Western societies are still grappling with poverty, inequality, and violence. And we can't seem to make any progress in addressing long-term collective issues such as global warming and environmental destruction. There seems to be no better political and moral philosophy than liberalism, yet our world faces an existential threat.

In the magazine *Tricycle*, Buddhist scholar Stephen Batchelor interrogated us:

> Do we really want to be complicit in a consumerist lifestyle that is driving thousands of species to extinction? Do we wish to be part of an economic system that condemns millions of people to repetitive, meaningless work? Do we need even a fraction of the items we are daily encouraged to purchase, briefly enjoy, then discard? Do we like living in a world where a tiny minority control most of its resources and wealth, condemning millions to social exclusion and poverty? Do we want to contribute to making this planet uninhabitable each time we board another long flight to an overhyped tourist destination? If the answer to these questions is no,

then we face the most challenging question of all: *How are we to live together in this world?*

The solutions will be collective, not individual. Leaders, from the most powerful to the most modest, must lead this collective effort. It is the only path toward a fairer, more compassionate, and sustainable world. This is a matter of survival, if not for us, then for our children.

Leaders have one of the most difficult roles in the world. They chart a journey and inspire their followers. Together, they can fulfill their vision. It doesn't matter whether the purpose is for profit or not. All forms of leadership require vision, courage, energy, and interpersonal skills.

THE INVITATION TO AN INNER JOURNEY

Contemplative leadership is the gateway to building coherence between our inner wisdom and our actions in the world. We develop greater presence, balance, and clarity about why and how we lead. We don't only use our head to track performance indicators. We engage our whole self—mind, body, and heart—to tap into our deepest resources.

Father Laurence Freeman exemplifies this journey. A Benedictine monk, he is both a leader and a contemplative. He leads a global organization, the World Community for Christian Meditation, with members in a hundred countries. He also heads the Abbey of Bonnevaux in France, where a Benedictine community was first established in the twelfth century. I asked Laurence to share how he invites CEOS, government leaders, and all types of people into the inner journey. His words showcase just how important retreats can be—whether for a few moments during the course of a day or for an extended getaway. Here's what he shared with me:

I have been a monk for more than thirty years. I have learned—it's part of the wisdom in monastic life—that relationship with others at a deep, transparent level is vital to a healthy human life. But solitude is also necessary to develop healthy relationships.

Over the years, leading the World Community for Christian Meditation and, recently, our new center at Bonnevaux has taught me that leadership, although hard, is meant to be good, fulfilling, and useful work. My definition of "good work" is what brings out the best in us and is of benefit to others. As meditation is part of my life's work, personally and through teaching, I have come to see that meditation, too, is good work and helps make all our work better.

Whether you are a monk or not, the danger is that work becomes an obsessive, uncontrollable tyrant demanding more and more from you and becoming less and less satisfying or personally enjoyable. This is particularly true when we have too much ego and ambition invested in it. If that happened, meditation helps reduce the ego factor and restore the joy.

This is why a leader needs to be disciplined about taking time away from work. It's called "detachment." If we don't, if we are constantly involved in problem-solving and monitoring everything, we lose perspective. This affects not only the quality of the work itself, but also inflates our ego, which gets hooked in a spiral of megalomania and paranoia. Look at the end of political tyrants. We think that everything revolves around me and depends entirely on me, forgetting how everything is interdependent. Relationships with colleagues are sucked into a black hole by our own lack of solitude and detachment.

My daily life is busy. St. Benedict said, "Idleness is the enemy of the soul." But it is punctuated by regular short times of prayer and meditation stepping back from the busyness: at fixed times, morning, midday, and evening. If I am involved in something and almost finishing it, it can feel an intrusion to drop it and go to meditate. But I never regret it. These times are like mini retreats, which is easier for me because I am living a monastic life. But increasingly people living more conventional lives do the same and benefit.

We need to be precise about these times for being rather than doing and learn to be faithful to them. Energetic people with active minds who are attached to the outcome of their work will feel a stab of anxiety when they step away from it into stillness and silence. Whether it is for twenty minutes of meditation or a full retreat, however, the rewards are great—for ourselves and our work.

It doesn't matter how responsible, high up the ladder we are. When the interior bell strikes, calling you to meditation or time away, listen and respond. This builds a natural discipline that bears much fruit.

My own experience of retreats is that each day needs a conscious effort of detachment and solitude from what we are doing. Not checking messages, not problem-solving. Trusting. We then come back to our work with freshness of vigor and hope because we have unhooked the attachments that can hook us with anxiety or distraction. In the monastic community I am responsible to, we meditate together and doing that on a regular basis, whatever your lifestyle, is very encouraging. I can see that in the members of our Bonnevaux Business group that meets online each week.

Longer retreats, away from the familiar workplace and home and from the people we usually live and work with are also very beneficial. As we speak, I am taking an extended retreat in my hermitage but staying in Zoom contact with my local and extended community. Absence makes the heart fonder!

Retreats cure loneliness with solitude. There is inevitable loneliness in leadership. Having the top job, with all its responsibilities, creates distance and projection. The place where the buck stops can become lonely. The best cure for loneliness is solitude, which we can find in the retreats and also in our daily meditation. Solitude is the discovery and acceptance of our uniqueness. Loneliness is failed solitude.

To help leaders, I often skip the factual "benefits" of meditation and stress the "fruits." No one is going to be persuaded to meditate by statistics and scientific evidence. Leaders meditate or give themselves to retreats when they know they need it. Sometimes an invitation or suggestion can awaken that. More than scientific research, texts from the wisdom traditions can often be that invitation. Because I teach in an inclusive, ecumenical way we choose texts from different traditions—Buddhist, Sufi, Christian, native traditions. Today, whether I am addressing business leaders, doctors, or MBA students, most of them are secular, nonreligiously aligned. But people respond well to wisdom texts and to silence. We take a short text, share our responses, and meditate together. I also recommend that to refresh and sustain their practice, busy people under pressure keep spiritual texts near them.

Sometimes, I meet former students who show off a well-thumbed copy of one of these books. The results of meditation are also perceptible! It's quite easy to see whether someone is keeping up their practice.

It's true. The results are obvious. But to reach those results, we must first acknowledge our full selves. We must move toward alignment.

THE THREE CENTERS

We cannot be effective leaders when we are fragmented. We cannot ignore the fundamental alignment between our three centers of intelligence: mind, heart, and body. Sometimes, our bodies are in the meeting room, but our minds are elsewhere. We force ourselves to complete a project, but "our heart is not in it." Or we work day and night, ignoring the impact that this will have on our health.

When the three centers are not aligned, you're incapable of coherent action. This is what happened to Susan. She knew something was missing, but she couldn't name it. An unacknowledged part of her, long ignored, had now decided it was time to emerge.

The ultimate purpose of the contemplative inner journey is to reconnect our three centers. This is easier said than done when hyperactivity is our standard.

The Indian sage Ramana Maharshi allegedly said: "Your own Self-Realization is the greatest service you can render the world." Regaining alignment through contemplation is a step toward this realization.

So, let's embark together on this inner journey of self-discovery. Retreats are the cradle for this adventure into stillness. You can silence your critical voice right from the onset. This won't be a self-improvement course, and you will soon realize that you were whole since the beginning. There are no deficiencies to fix.

No self-improvement visualization. Only an invitation to curiosity and discovery.

THE MAGICAL ISLAND

Nothing has prepared us for the inner journey. Many of us reach adulthood with skills to navigate only the outer world. Our schools and universities teach us all there is to know about science, business, and humanities. But no one explained to us how our mind, emotions, and physiology interconnect. All we know is how to achieve a never-ending series of targets. We learn the rules of society and get good grades. We get a degree, a job, and a promotion. We get married, buy a house, and produce kids. The cycle can repeat itself. We get better at navigating the external world, yet we don't have a map of our inner world.

When we're always in pursuit of a new achievement, the game never stops. We are like the mountain climbers who reach a summit only to realize that there is a higher peak, hidden from the first one that must now be climbed.

We keep telling ourselves, "I'll be happy when…" stories: "I'll be happy when I get promoted." "I'll be happy when I get married." "I'll be happy when I launch this new product." "I'll be happy when sales reach one hundred million." "I'll be happy when I buy a new house." The problem with these stories is that reaching the coveted milestone only reveals a new "I'll be happy when" story.

One of my teachers, Steve March, calls this narrative "the magical island where it all turns out." This narrative prevents us from enjoying the present moment, which, after all, is the only reality we have. Happiness is somewhere in a hypothetical future. We swim and swim and don't notice that like a mirage, the magical island keeps getting further and further. Life becomes a succession of milestones. We don't realize that the game never ends.

My friend Subba is a retired banker who is now a spiritual teacher and retreat leader. He is one of the few people I know who knows how to pause the game and truly see with clarity. More than fifteen years ago, Subba inspired me to undertake personal retreats. Every Christmas, Subba locks himself in a room for four days to find clarity and purpose in stillness. He told me:

Every year, I look forward to these retreats. The biggest benefit is that for a few days, I have nothing to do. It's an open slate. Every day, we live with a to-do list. So, a retreat is a nothing-to-do list, a clean slate. This is beautiful. The fact that I have the freedom not to do anything is amazing. We say we have free will. A retreat is a "free won't," the freedom not to.

The second beautiful thing that I experience on a retreat is that I get to be my BFF, my best friend forever. I can be nonjudgmental, understanding, and present for myself. That is amazing because I know that I can open up and I can relax. The third benefit is the serendipity, the beauty, the surprise. I don't plan what happens during a retreat. What experience is going to show up? This anticipation is enjoyable. I never experience boredom; there's so much to explore. It's like a new world and so exciting.

We are so fascinated by the magical island, the elusive destination, that we don't want to face the journey. Our lives become a self-improvement reality show. There is always something to fix, and we are the experts at problem-solving.

Spiritual traditions teach us how misguided these views are. We see through contemplation, like Subba does each year, that we are already whole—if only we would remove the layers of ignorance that veil our eyes. As Buddhists say, we are all potential Buddhas. Like the acorn, we only need the right amount of shade, sun, and rain to grow into an oak tree.

RETREAT TRADITIONS

First, a definition. A retreat is about taking time to immerse ourselves in stillness and silence. A retreat can last years or two hours. We will explore the structure of retreats in detail in the next chapter.

Retreats originate from and play a central role in spiritual traditions. As a leader, you can use what these traditions have to teach so you, too, can connect Doing and Being.

In spiritual traditions, retreats connect the seekers to their quest, be it God, Nirvana, Liberation, or the Ultimate Truth. The retreat is a time to set aside our worldly concerns. Sometimes, the seeker—for example, a recluse or hermit—will remain in retreat mode for years. Some traditions, like Buddhism, emphasize the importance of regular retreats. In Tibetan and Bhutanese lineages, novice monks undergo a three-year retreat. It is a rite of passage into adulthood before receiving full ordination.

A few years ago, my wife and I hosted a young Bhutanese monk, Nima, in our Singapore home. Nima was taking a crash course in technology so he could install computers in his monastery. He explained to us that in Bhutan, monks undergo a three-year retreat to test their vocation. The discipline is tight. Monks-in-training spend many hours a day meditating in silence. Most novices look forward to that period of introspection and reflection. "It is what allows us to get to know ourselves, and to confirm that this is the life we want to live," he explained. "How could we lead communities otherwise?"

As I researched the art of retreats more, I found that many spiritual traditions encourage their practitioners to spend time in regular contemplation. The training of Jesuit priests can take up to fifteen years and includes several retreats. The novice Jesuit will perform spiritual exercises scripted in the sixteenth century by the founder of the order, St. Ignatius de Loyola.

Retreats can be rites of passage. Young men in Thailand take temporary ordination during a rainy season. In India, following Hindu tradition, householders retire from world affairs and find a place to live a simpler life in the forest. According to Christian tradition, Jesus retreated to the desert where he fasted for forty days. This was his way of strengthening his discipline and preparing for his work of salvation. His example inspired the Desert Fathers. These early Christians retreated into the Egyptian desert. There, they prayed and lived simple lives. Their example inspired the first monastic orders.

Finally, retreats act as regular markers of time in many traditions. For example, in Judaism, Shabbat is the weekly time taken to rest and pray after six days of work. There's also Ramadan in Islam and Lent in Christianity, both annual fasting retreats.

INTROSPECTION AS A
LEADERSHIP PRACTICE

In every society, lay people and contemplatives used to live together. Contemplatives inspired, and lay people supported them. In our modern secular culture, contemplative traditions are rarely honored in society and government. Our modern management science focuses on the supremacy of the mind. It ignores the role of spirituality in creating meaning and concentrates on building a rational, quantifiable approach to problem-solving. There is no place in the science of leadership for developing a rich inner life.

That was how it seemed, at least, until Daniel Goleman published *Emotional Intelligence* in 1995. Goleman had studied in India with spiritual leaders like Neem Karoli Baba. These leaders influenced his thinking on marrying leadership with introspection and meditation. For the first time, turning inward became recognized as a discipline to strengthen one's leadership skills.

Since then, scientists have researched the benefits of introspection for leaders. Psychologists, medical doctors, and business researchers have studied with contemplatives and practiced meditation. Some progressive companies have even adopted the practice to kick off their meetings.

Meditation is the practice of stilling and concentrating the mind. It allows us to achieve penetrating insights into the nature of our minds and reality. You do not need to practice meditation on your retreats. It is not the cure-all that some enthusiasts proclaim. But it can be a useful complement. I will suggest several meditation techniques in this book.

Likewise, you do not need to adhere to a spiritual tradition to schedule retreats. I often quote spiritual teachers, but I don't advocate in favor of a particular worldview. You can retreat without subscribing to any single religion or dogma.

THE RETREAT MANIFESTO

By retreating, leaders make a choice that is bold and counterintuitive. Here is a manifesto that summarizes the fundamental pillars of contemplative retreats.

First, by retreating, *I reject the narrative of busyness.* I do not justify my value based on the number of hours I spend in meetings or emails I send every week. I do not believe we always make the best decisions in the heat of the action. Retreats allow me to slow down, develop a new perspective, and take care of myself. As a reflective leader, I can be in turn busy and idle. I can be fast and slow, passionate and still, energized and calm, vocal and silent.

Second, *I appreciate my inner world.* I do not pretend that I am an invincible hero with no weaknesses, doubts, and vulnerabilities. I have emotions and feelings and a rich inner world. I can use it as a resource. As a contemplative leader, I can connect to my outer and inner worlds. Retreats provide me with a space to quiet my mind, reflect, and tap into my inner wisdom.

Third, *I acknowledge that leadership and solitude are complementary, not opposite.* The success of my actions depends on my ability to influence a wide range of stakeholders. Solitude allows me to put my relationships in perspective. I can develop greater empathy and compassion for others and myself. As a contemplative leader, I can value solitude and company at the same time.

In his *Pensées*, French philosopher Blaise Pascal reflected: "When I have occasionally set myself to consider the different distractions of men, the pains and perils to which they expose themselves at court or in war, whence arise so many quarrels, passions, bold and often bad ventures, etc., I have discovered that all the unhappiness of men arises from one single fact, that they cannot stay quietly in their own chamber."

Again, the path of retreats reconciles the seemingly opposing worlds of leadership and contemplation so that we will not fall prey to these pains and perils. The Isha Upanishad showed us the way three thousand years ago:

In the dark night live those for whom the world without alone is real; in night darker still, for whom the world within alone is real. The first leads to a life of action, the second to a life of meditation. But those who combine action with meditation cross the sea of death through action and enter into immortality through the practice of meditation. So have we heard from the wise.

Remember my client, Susan? When she eventually came back from the desert, she made a few important changes in her life. She negotiated to work four days a week. This freed time for activities that were meaningful for her and gave her greater balance. She started reading and exercising again. She found time for reflection. She learned to slow down and connect mind and body. In short, she found the essence of contemplation and applied it to her life.

When I saw her recently, she told me that she was living life with wisdom and curiosity. For Susan, a whole new journey has unfolded, and she now has the time and space to find her path. You can do the same.

ADDITIONAL JOURNALING
AND REFLECTIONS

In Chapter 4, I will introduce the practice of journaling. It is an important component of retreats. For now, buy yourself a beautiful notebook. You will take pleasure using it and rereading it for years. Do not use an electronic device. Stick to pen and paper, even though it makes writing slower. The intimate bond between writer, pen, and journal fosters introspection and minimizes distractions. And you need less electronics, not more.

We journal on questions that don't have yes or no answers. The questions become an object of meditation, which we can explore from many angles. It is like a koan, a riddle that Zen monks use to speed up their awakening. We are not seeking an answer, for there is no problem to solve. We only want to bask in the experience of contemplating the question.

Take your notebook, choose one of the following questions, and sit in silence for a few minutes. Be spontaneous and write what comes to mind.

- What are the roots of my busyness?
- What are my fears about not being busy?
- If I had more time, what would I do with it?
- Can I differentiate between time that I control vs. time that is controlled for me?
- How would I spend my life if there were no expectations?

- What would become possible if I were less busy? If I saw more clearly? If I were more balanced? If I knew my purpose?

Now that we have examined the *why* of retreats, let's move to the *how*. In the next chapter, we will explore the four pillars of retreats.

Chapter 3

THE FOUR PILLARS
of a RETREAT

W HILE RETREATS ORIGINATED WITHIN SPIRITUAL traditions, they can certainly be used as a gateway to contemplative leadership. They create the conditions for peace and stillness and deep, reflective thought.

Contemplation is the antidote to the three poisons of modern leadership: fragmentation, pressure, and complexity. How can we expect to face critical dilemmas or make important decisions when we are agitated and rushed? How can we think amidst incessant noise? When we engage in contemplation, we insert a space between the conditions we face and the actions we take. We reclaim the clarity, balance, and purpose that allow us to make conscious choices. We see how to do our part in creating a better world.

Still, many leaders are reluctant to carve out quality time to reflect on their action in the world. They feel time-starved. When I suggest retreats to my clients, many of them think they couldn't possibly add one into their busy schedules with work and family. And the perspective of spending time alone is daunting.

THE COMPONENTS OF A RETREAT

But are retreats truly so impossible for leaders? Let's return to the definition. Remember, a retreat is simply time set aside to contemplate and develop fresh perspectives. We do this in silence, in solitude, in an inspiring space, and with the intention to connect to the spirit. I use "spirit" here without religious connotations. It only indicates that we have an inner compass, born out of our conditions and character. We can think of these components as the Four Ss: Silence, Solitude, Space, and Spirit.

Silence

Modern societies are noisy. We don't realize it until we experience silence for an extended period. I live in the city and barely notice the ambient noise anymore. Cars, trucks, and motorbikes. Construction sites, public transport, and music in every store and restaurant.

I sometimes hold workshops for leaders and ask my participants questions about their daily lives. For example, I'll say:

"You're outside in the street and receive an important phone call. Where do you go to find silence to take your call?" Participants scratch their heads. There is rarely an obvious answer.

Even inside, our open-floor offices are noisy. Conversations, phones ringing, colleagues raising their voice while on a conference call. Studies show that productivity drops when office workers cannot isolate themselves to think. Working from home during the COVID pandemic has been beneficial for our concentration and productivity.

Finally, our devices, even when they are set in silent mode, are a major source of physical and mental noise. Notifications compete for our attention and remind us that messages are waiting. They create a sense of urgency that is impossible to resist.

Many executives have confessed that they do their best thinking on long-haul flights. No interruptions, no signal, no distractions. They liken these flights to a retreat in the skies.

Silence is about leaving all this agitation behind. Silence is of course figurative: we are not seeking the impossible absence of sounds. We want to eliminate distractions, disturbances, and noise pollution. These, according to studies, lead to stress, poor concentration, and fatigue.

On the contrary, soft sounds, like waves crashing on the beach or a forest teeming with life, support reflection wonderfully. In a city, we can look for the soft ambience of a hotel lobby or a quiet coffee shop. With a coffee in front of you, you can consider yourself in retreat land!

The first step toward silence is turning off devices or setting them to airplane mode. Even a short digital detox can be daunting at first. We are suddenly free to experience our thoughts without distraction.

Silence opens the door to a wonderful place that we rarely visit. Perhaps we've experienced it when walking alone in nature, watching a sunset, or stargazing.

In those moments of silence, we can finally reconnect with ourselves. We connect with our thoughts, feelings, and sensations. Constant noise and connectivity are only a recent phenomenon in the much longer timescale of human evolution. And silence is a channel to rediscover our humanity. As we scrape away the chaotic layers of modern life, we regain our true nature.

Solitude

Solitude and silence complement each other. Like silence, solitude can be figurative more than literal. On a retreat, we do not need to eliminate interactions with others. We seek the absence of distractions more than the absence of other human beings.

As Father Laurence highlighted, we often confuse solitude with loneliness. While loneliness is an undesirable condition, solitude is a luxury. Many leaders are lonely, but they rarely find solitude. Solitude is a precondition for contemplation. Some seek it, and others are afraid of it. This is a result of our conditioning and character. Introverts seek quiet moments to recharge their batteries and analyze situations in depth.

Extroverts derive their energy and necessary stimulation from social interaction.

The traits of extroversion—action orientation, friendliness, enthusiasm, and sociability—are often associated with leadership. No wonder many leaders balk at the idea of spending quiet time reflecting. They prefer in-the-moment decisions. In an era when working in teams is a virtue, the suggestion that we might be more productive alone is almost sacrilegious. Studies, however, show that we do our best thinking alone, not in a group. Whether we are writing a speech or developing a vision, we must first reflect alone before sharing and getting feedback. In solitude, with no distractions, we can take a relaxed yet alert stance toward the issues we want to tackle.

Solitude, unlike loneliness, doesn't happen by accident. It results from a deliberate decision to fight the urge to interact with others. This is why these long-haul flights have become the last refuge for senior executives. They can enjoy a meeting-free schedule without appearing to be slacking.

Finally, silence and solitude are necessary for decision-making. Leaders are often subject to doubt. In the face of the most difficult decisions, they are often torn. When experts are no longer useful and when colleagues have stated their views, it is the leader's role to choose a course of action. Doubts and questions about legitimacy arise: Am I qualified to decide? Should I be responsible for such a complex endeavor, or am I an impostor? It is in solitude and silence, in the narrow channel between Doing and Being, that leaders often draw on their deepest resources and find courage and resolve to overcome doubt.

Space

You are sensitive to your environment in ways you sometimes don't notice or understand. Some spaces immediately improve your mood and lift your spirits. Others make you feel oppressed and uncomfortable. This is true for homes and offices and for places you only pass through: a vacation resort, airplane cabin, or restaurant. Without noticing, you react to aesthetics, clutter, sounds, smells, and light. You can walk into a hotel room and immediately feel drained. You house-hunt and fall in love with a property at first sight. Research has shown that beautiful spaces support psychological and emotional wellness. I call it "feeling the vibe" of a space.

Perhaps there is a special place that inspires you. I love a quaint village in the Spanish mountains. It overlooks the arid plains of Extremadura and has its back against the imposing Gredos mountain range. My village may not be the most picturesque, but I love retreating there every summer. The proximity to nature slows my urge to be active. My pace eases when I walk in the woods or swim in the icy cold streams. I can read a book at one of the many cafes with a cerveza in front of me. This is a place where I love to reflect, meditate, write, read, and simply relax.

Our retreats should ideally include time in Mother Nature, which gives us life. Since we split from the chimps six million years ago, we spent all but the last two hundred years in close contact with nature. We are not hardwired to thrive indoors in asphalt jungles. It should not come as a surprise that increasing our exposure to nature durably improves our mood. We can spend time in parks, gardens, or forests. Researchers studied the Japanese practice of forest bathing. They found that participants exhibited lower levels of stress, decreased sympathetic nervous activity, and reduced heart rate and blood pressure. Living in leafy communities, walking in the woods, or gardening are similarly positive. These activities bring mood improvement and increased cognitive functions. Nature makes us smarter and more balanced.

That said, a connection with nature is not a prerequisite for a successful retreat as long as we can settle comfortably with our senses at peace. I have done many retreats in urban settings—at home, in a comfortable hotel room, or in a cozy coffee shop. The comfort of our own homes is often the easiest way to get started, as we don't need to worry about logistics. Even in urban retreats, the noise quickly vanishes in the background if we can concentrate on the space around us. Urban walks are a lovely way to reflect and disconnect. Many cities offer peaceful walking circuits through parks, calm streets, or riverbanks.

Your intuition will guide you toward the spaces that resonate with you and are the most conducive for your retreats. I encourage my clients to use their imagination and explore where they could spend a few hours or a few days in silence and solitude.

Flying to Bali or Costa Rica may not guarantee a contemplative retreat. The stress of traveling to a foreign country and the jetlag can offset the benefit of a beautiful space. A familiar, comfortable place or a simple rented cabin within a few hours' drive will work.

Ultimately, the ideal retreat space allows you to feel safe, at peace, and comfortable. It is not about gaining followers on Instagram. Instead, you need to ensure you can be free of interruptions and interactions for the duration of your retreat. You can do this best by finding an inspiring space to enjoy silence and solitude.

Spirit

The last element of a retreat is the spirit. Spirit is another word for soul, and I often use the two interchangeably. However, soul may be associated with religion, which is not my intention. There is no requirement to believe in an eternal soul. The spirit is our inner world, which goes beyond the logic of the mind.

This inner world is where we experience intuition, emotions, feelings, and moods. It is where we experience interoception and proprioception. Interoception is the sense of the internal state of our body. This includes our main organs, like the heart, skin, or stomach. Proprioception is the awareness of our body in space. It allows us to move around a room or touch an object with our eyes closed. These felt senses allow us to perceive our own embodiment and connect it with heart and mind. We rarely acknowledge our connection to the spirit, but we frequently use sentences like "I don't feel it..." or "I have a hunch..." or "My gut tells me that..."

The spirit is the glue that gives us our individual and collective humanity. We can observe the spirit when we acknowledge that our brains, hearts, and bodies are not separate devices that operate independently. Instead, they are intimately connected. We also observe our spirit when we recognize that we are not isolated beings but connected to one another across space and time, and to our environment.

Let's illustrate some of these interconnections. Consider the anger that arises when someone crosses your physical or conceptual boundaries. A part of you gets triggered and you experience the emotion of anger. This anger manifests itself in your physiology. Your heart rate and blood pressure increase. Your body tenses up, and you clench your teeth.

In the other direction, a physical discomfort—one so small that you may not notice initially, like sitting on an uncomfortable chair—can trigger negative emotions and thoughts. Or you may feel particularly calm and tolerant after a relaxing massage.

We can observe our interconnection with other beings, past, present, and future, human and nonhuman alike. We owe our lives to all the generations that have preceded us. We speak languages that distant ancestors developed and refined. The clothes we wear, the food we eat, the cars we drive, are the product of thousands, if not millions, of individuals, each doing a small part of the work. Our default mode of existence is tribal. In isolation, in loneliness, we die. Not only do we miss interactions with other humans, but we also cannot guarantee our safety and shelter.

My friend Stéphane provided a beautiful illustration of this connection to the spirit through his regular retreats. Stéphane, who worked at prestigious banks like Goldman Sachs and UBS, needs to retreat to make sense of the changes in his life. He explains:

It is the place where I have been going back to and finding shelter all my life. It is a house lost in the green and deep countryside of Auvergne in the French Massif Central—quite difficult to find but not impossible to reach once you know the path: I can be there for lunch on Friday provided I leave my house in Singapore before midnight on Thursday.

When I make the choice of going, it undoubtedly carries the meaning to taking myself off the grid, a rare and passing moment in life when I completely disconnect from business and networks. A happy few of close friends and family would reach me there, and only a small circle of longtime friends will ever get a laissez-passer.

I have come to experience the time in Pranal as a lapse of time after and/or before action and race. Time flows more slowly there, and I have gone there on the eve of a big decision I had to make in my life, or after a big event or an important turn.

My big decisions (relationships, marriage, moving to new cities or new continent, making important changes to my career) were made in the calm and the serenity of that house. It is a very special place for me.

To be sure, I have found myself completely alone there for days at times. These are the real moments of true retreat in the pure definition of the term. I have enjoyed the complete silence, the wind in the trees outside, the cracks of the fire in the chimney inside, the ding-dong of the old clock with every passing hour. But silence does not define me, as I like to put on a record, like Ennio Morricone's *Ecstasy of Gold* or Ryuichi Sakamoto's *Merry Christmas Mr. Lawrence*. With tunes like these, and playing old vinyl records, I take the time to stop, breathe, and think in this ambiance. This is no solitude, more like a certain detachment. My whole experience is very meditative.

There is no retreat without an openness and desire to connect to spirit. We want to know ourselves better and explore the connection between mind, heart, and body. Curiosity must be the driving force behind a retreat. The more we explore, the more we realize how little we know.

Jesuit priest Pierre Teilhard de Chardin once said: "We are not human beings having a spiritual experience. We are spiritual beings having a human experience." We can confirm this every day. Your mind may push you in a direction, but your spirit tells you something else. I've seen this truth play out over and over again with my clients.

Louisa, the chief economist at an investment bank, told me how she moved up the ranks in her career but deep down aspires to find harmony and peace in her life. She explained, "My dream would be to be a number two, away from the light and the pressure. And here I am, presenting my team's analysis of the markets to heads of central bank and finance ministers."

Salman, who heads up the regional investment team for a private equity firm, makes his points forcefully and often interrupts others without noticing. "Ideas come to me so rapidly that I can't speak fast enough to express them," he told me. "I really don't mean to cut off my subordinates, but I feel almost physically uncomfortable when the discussion escapes me." Deep down, Salman admits he fears being controlled by others and knows there's a better way.

Erica, a cerebral New Yorker and partner at a law firm, has become a global expert in sustainability. Yet she still struggles to find her purpose in life despite the success she has achieved professionally. She opened up and confessed, "I haven't found my purpose. I thought I had, for many years, when I kept getting promoted. Now I just feel empty. I know it is not true, but it feels like my life has been stagnant for the last five years."

Superficial conversations or performance feedback will not help Louisa, Salman, or Erica. They are stuck despite their intelligence, capacity for hard work, and successful leadership. They all feel something deeper stirring, but only the openness to the spirit can unlock their unfoldment. For them and many other leaders, retreats provide the perfect setup for the deep inner work needed.

Now that you know the four pillars of retreats, it's time to get into specifics. In the next chapter, we'll look at what exactly you might do on your retreat.

ADDITIONAL JOURNALING AND REFLECTIONS

Take one question that inspires you and stay with it for a few days or a week. Notice how your answers may evolve as you explore each layer of your experience.

- When and where do I find silence? What do I like and what scares me about silence?
- When and where do I find solitude? What is, for me, the difference between solitude and loneliness? What do I like and what scares me about solitude?
- Which spaces inspire me? What makes them so inspiring? How do I show up differently in an inspiring space?
- What does connecting with my spirit mean to me? How do I do it? What does this do for me?

Chapter 4

DESIGNING *a* RETREAT

THE FOUR PILLARS OF A RETREAT—SILENCE, SOLI-tude, Space, and Spirit—provide the solid foundation for a successful retreat experience. But what exactly happens on a retreat?

I advocate a simple principle: you cannot have a fulfilling retreat experience if you are not looking forward to it. And you cannot look forward to a retreat if it doesn't bring you peace and joy. A retreat, first and foremost, is a treat. You can choose to adopt strict rules and schedules, or you may simply let go, with no specific agenda. A retreat's first objective is to reconnect with yourself. You can design it to suit your natural and personal rhythms.

For example, I schedule writing and reflecting in the morning when my brain is awake and sharp. I do walks or daydreaming when my attention is less focused. I follow my heart, too. On a blue-sky morning, the cool air inspires me to sit and contemplate nature for a while. On a rainy day, I will stay indoors and read. Some planning is good, but it's not necessary to script an hour-by-hour schedule. Particularly on your first retreats, you will need to find your own pace.

When I first started taking retreats, I made the mistake of overplanning. I felt stressed when I fell behind schedule. At one point, I realized that this was worse than being at work, so I threw my schedule away. Letting go of what we believe we must "achieve" is an important discovery on our first retreats. When we walk in nature, we don't know what meadow will call us for a nap, what path will invite our exploration, or what country pub will entice us for a refreshment.

RETREAT ACTIVITIES

All of that said, I advise having a general idea of how you want to use your precious retreat time. The hours can be structured in various segments depending on the goal of the retreat. Here is a nonexhaustive list of possible activities:

1. Contemplation (prayer, meditation, and daydreaming).
2. Journaling.

3. Reflecting.

4. Reading.

5. Creative activities.

6. Walks.

7. Meals.

8. Sleep.

9. Rituals.

Let's examine them one by one.

Contemplation: Prayer, Meditation, and Daydreaming

American Trappist monk Thomas Merton provides a wonderful definition of contemplation in the opening of his memoir *New Seeds of Contemplation*:

> Contemplation is the highest expression of our intellectual and spiritual life. It is that life itself, fully awake, fully active, fully aware that it is alive. It is spiritual wonder. It is spontaneous awe at the sacredness of life, of being. It is gratitude for life, for awareness and for being. It is a vivid realization of the fact that life and being in us proceed from an invisible, transcendent, and infinitely abundant source. Contemplation is, above all, awareness of the reality of that source. It knows that source, obscurely, inexplicably, but with a certitude that goes both beyond reason and beyond simple faith.

In contemplation, we open to the possibility of directing our attention inward. This is not always an intuitive endeavor for leaders used to dealing with the outer world. To do so, we must reduce external stimulation and distraction and tune in to our thoughts, feelings, emotions, and physical sensations.

There are many forms of contemplations and many gateways we can walk through. Prayer is a common form of contemplative activity. The secular practices of meditation and mindfulness are alternatives that do not entail a connection with a higher being. They invite us to simply be and notice what is in the present moment—with curiosity and without reacting or judging.

These practices offer the contemplative leader an escape from the reactiveness of daily life. They help create a space of freedom between stimulus and reaction. When you step away from daily events, you elevate yourself. Like a general observing a battle-field from the top of a hill, you can appreciate the forces at work without being caught in them. Imperceptibly, you are no longer a subject fused with the action. Instead, your desires, feelings, and emotions become distinct objects. This shift from subject to object is a fundamental marker of personal growth.

When senior executives need to reflect on important deci-sions, I often suggest they spend time in contemplation. Short retreats act as an accelerator toward an expanded perspective. It is only when you distance yourself from the immediacy of your daily decisions that you can observe the longer-term impact of your actions.

Daydreaming, or idly following your thoughts, can also be included in the list of contemplative activities. The research on daydreaming is recent and suggests that the activity is a sign of a well-adjusted and active mind. Daydreaming also correlates with improved working memory and higher intelligence (although we don't know which comes first). If you find yourself lost in thought during a retreat, don't feel guilty.

Journaling

For some, journaling may evoke visions of Bridget Jones. For others, writing a journal is a privilege of the literarily gifted such as Virginia Woolf. Very few executives think of journaling as a critical leadership tool. Yet several research studies have documented its benefits. Social psychologist James Pennebaker showed that journaling increases memory; strengthens the immune system; and improves sleep, mood, and mindfulness. Keeping a journal also helps you make sense of your life.

Journaling simply entails writing down your experience on the contemplative path. No need to be a literary talent; the style is free, and you can write in prose, short sentences, bullet points, or doodles. I advise my clients to buy a nice notebook made of quality paper. It should be an object they will enjoy carrying with them, writing in, and rereading in the future.

I discourage electronic diaries for several reasons. First, we need less screen time. Second, the physical act of writing commits you to introspection because you create an intimate moment between yourself, your experience, and the recording of the experience. An imprint is created at that moment that will allow you to remember what you wrote. Typing on a keyboard cannot accomplish that.

Journaling hones your self-awareness. You turn within and write about your moods, thoughts, experience, nocturnal dreams, and the meaning you attribute to events. You narrate the intimate experience of your mind, heart, body, and spirit. You examine what happened and what you would have liked to happen, what is helping you, and what is hindering you. You recount interactions and how you felt about them. You capture images, ideas, desires, associations, and insights that come to you so you can return and explore them later.

I have been writing in diaries for years. I occasionally read old reflections and measure how much I've changed in some dimensions and how little I've changed in others. I am fascinated by the aspirations of my twenties and thirties that have become a reality many years later. For example, even though I was studying engineering, I was fascinated with human development. I started reading about Asian spiritual traditions years before I first traveled to the region. Journaling expresses the voice of the soul that you cannot hear any other way. Your future self will enjoy reading what you wrote six months, one year, or ten years before.

I encourage you to start a journal now. I promise you will thank me in the future. The best time to write is often in the morning when your egoistic defenses are still dormant. Write for five or ten minutes about whatever is on your mind, or write out your hopes and fears about the day to come. Let the stream of consciousness guide you. Enjoy the moment you spend with yourself.

Later in the book, I will offer additional journaling and reflection prompts to deepen your exploration in this area.

Reflecting

A retreat provides a conducive setting for reflection. Like meditation, reflection allows you to distance yourself from the day-to-day and develop a new perspective. Leaders refer to this practice in many ways: taking a step back, seeing the big picture, taking the view from the balcony. All these phrases evoke the idea of separating yourself from the combat zone.

When you slow down and find peace in stillness, your horizons expand and you develop a wider perspective. You enlarge your sphere of concern to include those whose voices are rarely heard. Your time horizon stretches, and you can now contemplate not only the next quarter but the next few years. You unleash your creativity and devise new solutions to old problems. You develop a sense of spaciousness, inclusiveness, and openness that you can tap into, again and again.

My friend, Ivan, an industrial engineer, does not practice meditation or prayer but loves to reflect in a quiet space. Every year, he flies to Vancouver Island and spends three days alone in a simple hotel facing the sea. This inspiring environment allows him to review the past year and set goals for the year ahead. In those quiet moments, he scrutinizes his soul and asks himself, "Am I on the right track? Is this what I am meant to do?"

Reading

Retreats are an ideal setting for reading. I sometimes dedicate an entire retreat to reading. I will bring two or three books with me and spend most of the day comfortably lounging on a balcony overlooking the beach.

In books, we find inspiration, knowledge, and ideas. It doesn't matter whether we read poetry, philosophy, novels, a spiritual classic, or a leadership book. Books are an endless source of wisdom accumulated over thousands of years.

Instead of choosing books, let the books choose you. When the disciple is ready, the teacher appears. Likewise, books will call you when you are ready. Have you ever had a book that sits on your shelves for years? You ignore it, finding no interest in it. Suddenly, one day you feel drawn to it. When this happens, it's worth taking up the invitation.

Creative Activities

You tap into different regions of your brain when you let your creative instincts flow. Drawing, painting, writing poetry, dancing, taking photographs, singing, or playing a musical instrument all invite you to let go of your analytical and logical side and connect with your spontaneous, imaginative, and intuitive power.

By tapping into your many talents, you create connections between reality and possibility. You connect the logical and analytical left brain to the creative and intuitive right brain. This holistic approach helps you in many aspects of your leadership, allowing you to embrace situations in their entirety.

Few leaders connect with their artistic gift. The professional life often leaves little space for beauty and aesthetics. To start in this area, it's helpful to remember your childhood and reconnect with your desire to create. What did you enjoy? Today, what moves you? Is it van Gogh's paintings, Wagner's operas, or Basho's poetry? On a retreat, there is always room to let art move us. With no one watching, start moving, drawing, singing, painting, or flowing with the rhythms of the drums or the flute. Invite beauty, inspiration, and flow to your retreat.

Walks

Walks offer movement and inspiration. It doesn't matter whether you walk around the park, along the beach, or the 600 miles of the Camino de Santiago—the famous pilgrimage route in Spain. You can walk with a plan or without aim, letting your heart decide which path to take. Along the way, you might find an inspiring spot and rest, taking in the sights, sounds, and smells.

Bring your journal along with you when you walk. There will almost always be a moment to capture the experience in writing instead of snapping a picture with your smartphone. Leaving the phone behind is the best way to shed the temptation to take pictures. Instead, you can just be present.

It's helpful to find outdoor places you want to explore. Walking in nature will demand the full engagement of your five senses. When there is no place to arrive, the journey becomes the destination. Every step contributes to the retreat.

Meals

A retreat can be the opportunity to shift your eating habits toward more conscious choices. You might decide to adopt a healthier diet after contemplation. During the retreat, while you are less active than usual, you need fewer calories. This may be the time to have smaller meals, or perhaps only take one or two meals a day, as you would if you retreated in a monastery.

It is only when you stop eating mechanically that you develop an awareness of your choices. Are you hungry, or are you just conditioned to eat on schedule? Slowing down also means that we can be mindful about every intake of food. Instead of wolfing down food between two appointments, take time to appreciate and chew every bite. The practice of mindful eating not only enhances your appreciation for food but also makes you eat less. Eating slowly means that you notice when you get full and stop. A useful trick is to put down your fork or spoon until you have finished swallowing the previous bite instead of mindlessly preparing your next bite as soon as you have shoved the previous one in your mouth.

To avoid distractions and interruptions, it is useful to plan your meals before the start of the retreat. You can stock up, or if you're like me and your cooking skills are nonexistent, you can arrange delivery, takeout or visits to restaurants while minimizing interactions and distractions.

Keep in mind that a retreat is a treat, not a punishment. If your regimen is too strict, you may give up or never retry. Finding the right balance between discipline and enjoyment is key to a successful retreat experience. We are retreatants, not penitents.

Sleep

On a retreat that extends over several days, listen to your body and sleep when you are tired. Most leaders have a chronic sleep deficit, and it is not uncommon to sleep long hours at the start of a retreat.

Slowing down in silence and solitude allows you to reconnect with your natural rhythms. Sleep is the victim of our modern lifestyle. Sleep time is short and often disrupted by stress or anxiety. You face long commutes, too much screen time, conference calls around the clock, and jetlag. Research shows that lack of sleep affects your cognitive performance. Your decision-making deteriorates as if you were under the influence of alcohol.

Sleep is important for many reasons, one being that it is the theater of your dreams. These visitors of the night tell you about your inner world. Listen to your dreams. Write them in your journal as soon as you wake up, without interpreting or analyzing.

What was your mood? Was there fear, anxiety, or optimism? Let the dreams speak to you. Dreams are a direct connection to the spirit. What is the dream trying to tell you? Why did it invite itself to your night?

On a retreat, you can reconnect with your natural sleep patterns. I enjoy the early morning hours for meditation, contact with nature, and journaling. And I never miss an opportunity to nap.

Depending on the season, you may find inspiration in following the rhythms of nature and rising with the sun. When I lead a retreat, I often schedule yoga and meditation at sunrise. We start in the dark, our meditation space only lit with candles. The only sounds we hear are crickets. As the hues of dawn lighten the sky, darkness turns into light and life. Birds start singing, roosters crow, and dogs bark in nearby villages. Finally, the sun appears at our backs, illuminating the nature in front of us. This is a profoundly spiritual experience for my participants and one of the most anticipated moments of their days, despite the 5:30 a.m. wake-up call.

Rituals

Finally, rituals are an integral part of our humanity and one of the ways we create a sense of purpose and belonging. Rituals connect us with the sacred. Practiced with others, rituals create community and shared meaning. Practiced alone, rituals help us get centered and facilitate our transition from the outer to the inner world.

Rituals are omnipresent. We often perform them long after we have forgotten their original significance. We celebrate birthdays, wedding anniversaries, and religious milestones like Christmas, even when we are not fervent practitioners.

Rituals are a gateway to the spirit. They are the small gestures that signify that we are leaving the world of agitation and material concerns behind and entering our sacred space of silence and solitude.

At the beginning of a retreat, a ritual symbolizes your intention to care for yourself, to embrace the topics you want to reflect on with an open heart, and to honor the answers that will come to you. Sitting down, centering yourself, and taking a few deep breaths can be enough to mark that transition. Perhaps you light a candle or the fireplace, symbolizing the light that is always guiding you.

At the closing, a ritual prepares you to transition back to the world. Sitting for a few moments, in gratitude for the opportunity to have this privileged time, you can vow to carry the benefits of the retreat back with you.

When I lead a group retreat, we celebrate the sunrise and sunset with a practice of meditation, breathing exercises, and yoga. This is a time to integrate mind, heart, and body, and sit in communion with nature. It is a time to recognize that despite our technology and intents to dominate the world, we are still creatures who lived with nature for eons, in awe of its rhythms and cycles.

The retreat itself can be a ritual. We might retreat during a full moon or a winter solstice, on anniversaries, or on religious holidays. Could you find a meaningful date to start your first retreat?

The next chapter will show you exactly how to get started.

ADDITIONAL JOURNALING
AND REFLECTIONS

- What are the rituals that give rhythm to my life?
- What questions am I asking myself?
- If I knew I had no limitation, what possibilities would open for me?
- If I knew I could spend two, four, or twenty-four hours uninterrupted, how would I spend my retreat time?

Mindfulness and Meditation

Mindfulness is a popular concept. It is often used as a secular substitute for meditation. However, there are fundamental differences between mindfulness and meditation.

Practicing mindfulness is simply directing your awareness to the present moment. You can be aware of your breath, physical sensations such as the movement of the air on your skin, or the taste and texture of a chocolate bar. You can also practice mindfulness when you walk, being attentive to every tiny action of your muscles producing the movement. You can be mindful of your thoughts. The list of objects of sustained attention is potentially endless. But the main three are physical sensations (the five senses), emotions or feelings, and thoughts.

Jon Kabat-Zinn is an American professor who adapted Eastern meditation techniques to the secular West. He defines mindfulness as the awareness that arises through paying attention, on purpose, in the present moment, nonjudgmentally, in the service of self-understanding and wisdom.

On a retreat, we practice mindfulness as we endeavor to bring our full attention to our experience, without judgment, and with an attitude of openness and curiosity. Many activities can be done with mindfulness, such as:

continued...

...continued

- *Eating and drinking (put down utensils between bites).*
- *Showering (enjoy the feeling of water on your skin).*
- *Walking (notice every movement of your legs and feet).*
- *Practicing yoga, tai chi, qigong, or any slow movement activity.*
- *Observing nature (sights, colors, sounds, smells) without naming or attaching labels.*
- *Drawing.*
- *Breathing or noticing body sensations.*
- *Thinking.*

In contrast, meditation is a deliberate practice of sitting in stillness. It can also be performed lying down or walking. You focus your attention on your breathing or choose other objects of attention, such as physical sensations, thoughts, or emotions. You notice what arises and let it pass. Your mind is like the infinite blue sky and your thoughts like passing clouds.

Meditation can also take the form of visualizations, such as feeling gratitude or sending well-wishes to yourself and others. In the second part of this book, we will explore several meditation techniques.

To practice meditation, you must be mindful, but you don't need to meditate to practice mindfulness!

Chapter 5

PRACTICAL
STEPS

E MMA IS A SENIOR HUMAN RESOURCES EXECUTIVE at a global defense contractor. Her company is publicly listed. Every day, she must navigate the tension between a corporate ethos focused on short-term profits and her desire to create a supportive and caring culture.

Emma has been with the company for fifteen years and has played the game long enough to know that there are no perfect solutions. To keep her balance, she takes regular breaks. She needs distance from the daily pressure to recharge and gain fresh perspective. She told me about her recent weeklong retreat on a small Greek island. "Above all else, I was looking for solitude, calm, and serenity," she told me. This was her experience in her own words:

The retreat project germinated slowly in my head. I shared it with my loved ones, and they were initially a little surprised. Why go alone? Isn't there enough room for them? I had to reassure them: I had nothing against them, but this was just something important for me. At the office, I didn't give any details, just that I was taking a week off. I did not want to explain; the choice to retreat alone was too personal.

Once I started my retreat, the days went by quickly. I felt immediately happy on my own, having breakfast, practicing yoga and meditation, jogging by the sea, walking on the beach enjoying the gentle October sun, away from the winter rain at home.

I always carried a book with me but hardly opened it. I wrote, dreamed, listened to music, and went with the flow. I created new habits and rituals, different and yet simply reassuring. Aware that this parenthesis was special, I enjoyed it with delight.

The texture of time also changed. Every morning, I wondered if I was going to find the day too long, and every day I savored every minute and found that time had both stretched out and passed very quickly.

I have rarely felt as alive as during this week.

Did I miss my loved ones? I must admit that I did not, even though we are a close-knit family. This was a moment just for myself, yet I did not feel selfish.

And as the week went on, I felt a growing clarity in my mind, in my plans, and in my life. It was at that point that I decided that I should build a house here, so I could return regularly.

I advise and lead retreats for senior leaders like Emma. These are successful individuals who have demonstrated discipline, resilience, and commitment throughout their careers. Yet, despite admitting that they need time for and by themselves, they often struggle to find time for a personal retreat.

Starting may be easier than you think.

STARTING SMALL

Let's distinguish same-day retreats from those that extend over at least one night.

It is wise to start small and schedule a short two-hour retreat to experience the power, and sometimes the challenges, of silence, solitude, space, and spirit.

As philosopher Jules Evans writes on his website, "A retreat can feel like a little death, coming down from the usual buzz of coffee-sugar-internet-gossip-ego-planning, and just sitting there… The ego may scream for distractions for the first day or two. 'Don't just sit there, do something!' But then things do settle down. And we discover a mind beyond the usual ego-chatter."

Be gentle on yourself as you begin this journey. Aim for short retreats until you are ready to experiment with longer ones. And even then, notice what comes up for you. Twenty years ago, I organized my first solo retreat in a beautiful tropical resort. My room was cozy, the grounds were spectacular, the pool inviting, the beach quiet. I had planned to spend three days meditating, reading, walking, and sleeping. Yet, after only a day and a half, I craved more stimulation. After an excruciating two days, I went home early. I learned two important lessons. First, a retreat is not a duration competition. Second, the ego puts up tremendous resistance to slowing down.

We react differently to the "stop doing" call. For some, disconnecting devices for two hours will be a challenge, while others love one week in the countryside with no Wi-Fi or neighbors. Find out what your starting point is.

Same-day retreats are the simplest to organize. They can take place at home, in nature, or in a calm public space that inspires you, like a public library or a museum! My favorite format for a short, peaceful interlude of contemplation is to spend a couple of hours in a coffee shop or a hotel lounge. I use these short breaks to open a new page in my journal and jot down ideas that come to my mind while sipping my coffee. I always return to the world feeling refreshed and inspired.

If you would like a longer retreat, consider starting in the later part of the afternoon and concluding before lunch the next day. Evenings and early mornings are particularly conducive to contemplation.

EXPLORING OUR RESISTANCE

We usually fail to disconnect because we don't have the tools to do so. Often, even though we feel legitimately entitled to a few hours or days by ourselves, we feel guilty about leaving work and family commitments behind.

The first person you will need to negotiate with is yourself. You may find numerous objections to taking time to retreat, including:

- I am too busy.
- I feel guilty taking time for myself.
- My business won't run without me.
- I don't want to face 1,000 emails when I come back.
- I am afraid to be alone.
- I don't have the discipline to block time for a retreat.
- This is a waste of time.
- I will be bored.
- What will others think?
- My partner will not understand.
- My weekends are reserved for my kids/golfing buddies/ running errands/cleaning the house.
- Others need me, and I can't disappear like that.

These objections are a symptom of our ideology of busyness and our modern lifestyle. They reflect a posture of helplessness:

"I would like to, but I can't." Rather than dismissing our resistance, we learn by exploring it. At the root often lies the fear of not being needed and the fear of facing ourselves.

When resistance arises, I ask my clients to explore the narrative unfolding in their head. Where does the fear come from? Is it legitimate? Or is it simply the reflection of a lifetime of habits? Are they in a position of power, feeling truly confident about the time allocation choices they make? Or are they feeling deflated and in a position of impotence? What hides behind the "I wish I could" or "I would love to, but I can't"?

Ultimately, resistance is a natural reaction. There is an opportunity for personal growth if we want to welcome this resistance and explore it with questions. What is holding me back? What am I afraid of? Unfortunately, we often choose to ignore the resistance and either grudgingly press ahead or cancel our retreat plans altogether. Take some time to sit with those questions and acknowledge why you feel so much resistance. Then choose how you will respond before you move forward to planning.

PRACTICAL STEPS

Here is a simple checklist to ensure that you are prepared for your retreat. It will help eliminate distractions. There is nothing worse than, once a retreat has started, to realize you forgot to bring a snack or a swimsuit. This list becomes even more important as you move on to longer retreats.

☐ Bookings (for the retreat place, cabin, hotel, or vacation rental).

☐ Tickets and transportation arrangements.

☐ Meal arrangements.

☐ Clearing the calendar and creating an out-of-office message.

☐ Ensuring that the works gets covered while away.

☐ Journal, notebook, pen, and paper.

☐ Phone, computer, and chargers (you may be offline and still want to listen to music).

☐ The book(s) you want to read.

☐ Comfortable clothing and layers adapted to the place of retreat.

☐ Exercise gear if needed (swimsuit, walking shoes, yoga mat, etc.).

☐ Toiletries and med kit.

☐ Food supplies, favorite coffee, tea, snacks.

☐ Insect repellent, sunscreen, a hat.

☐ Favorite ritual objects (I sometimes bring a candle with me).

Finally, it's important to share what you're doing with your loved ones. They, like Emma's family, may not necessarily understand at first. But over time, they'll see just how important retreats are for you. Each time I organize a retreat, I share my plans with my wife. Her support is important. She understands that these retreats benefit both of us, as I come back more peaceful, centered, and refreshed. I also block my calendar in advance, so my colleagues will not book appointments during these periods.

RETREAT TEMPLATES

I have prepared a few templates to inspire and guide you for your first retreats. Modify them as much as you want.

Remember to not pack your schedule. You don't want to feel rushed or pressured to complete your to-do list of meditation, walks, writing, reading, and yoga.

Let go of your busy leadership habits, your goals and objectives. This is not another day in the office but a sacred space that allows you to open to the unexpected and go with the flow of the day.

Leave plenty of empty slots to follow your inspiration and turn off all calendars and reminders.

A Short, Two-Hour Retreat

I love short retreats and take them regularly. The great thing about two-hour retreats is that you don't need to sacrifice much to squeeze them into your schedule, nor do they require much preparation. Yet the benefits are great, and pave the way for future deeper reflections.

A short retreat can be done at home when no one is around, in a park, a public library, on a short flight, or in a coffee shop. Your imagination is the limit!

FIRST TEN MINUTES

- Settling down.
- Getting the coffee or tea ready.
- Marking the beginning of the retreat with a small ritual:
    - Disconnecting devices.
    - Setting an intention for the retreat. For example, I want to regroup before an important meeting. Or I want to read this book and write down my thoughts in my journal. Or I want to process what has just happened to me.
    - Taking a few deep breaths to transition into retreat mode.
    - Making a commitment to silence, mindfulness, and seeking clarity and peace.

CORE OF THE RETREAT

- Sitting in silence and welcoming whatever comes up.
- Reading, writing, reflecting, journaling, meditating.
- If there is space, practicing qigong or yoga, breathing, crying, laughing, or, why not, just sleeping.

LAST TEN MINUTES

- Marking the end of the retreat with a small ritual:
  - Revisiting the initial intentions for the retreat. What unfolded?
  - Gratitude for this wonderful moment.
  - Commitment to keep the peace for as long as possible.
  - Commitment to the next retreat.

A Half-Day, Overnight Retreat

This is one of the simpler and most satisfying retreat formats. You can squeeze it in at the beginning of a weekend or even on a weekday, without disturbing the flow of life.

This retreat requires a comfortable place to sleep. It can be done at home or in a comfortable hotel in the city or a cabin in the countryside. Often, a change of landscape is all you need to break from conventional thinking habits.

This format is suitable to start reading and exploring the themes discussed in the second part of this book.

LATE AFTERNOON

5 p.m.–7 p.m.

- Settling down.

- Marking the beginning of the retreat with a small ritual:
  ○ Disconnecting devices.
  ○ Setting an intention for the retreat. For example, I want to start exploring one of the themes in Part II of this book. Or I want to slow down and reflect on my priorities for the next three months. Or I would like to take care of myself, without worrying constantly about others. Or I want an uninterrupted quiet time to take stock of my life.
  ○ Lighting a candle.
  ○ Making a commitment to silence, mindfulness, and seeking clarity and peace.
- Taking a moment to bask in the uninterrupted time that stretches in front of you. Suddenly, there are no deadlines, no clock, no rush, no appointments. You can just follow your natural inclinations and take your time with everything. Time opens in front of you.
- Reading, reflecting, and journaling.

EVENING

7 p.m.–9 p.m.

- Light dinner in silence and mindfulness, appreciating every bite.

- Mindful shower.
- Meditation or reading.

FIRST THING IN THE MORNING

- Meditation and yoga.
- Mindful shower.
- Reading, reflecting, and journaling.
- Light breakfast.

MID-MORNING

9 a.m.–11 a.m.

- Walk in nature.

BEFORE CLOSING THE RETREAT

11 a.m.–12 p.m.

- Reading, reflecting, and journaling.
- Marking the end of the retreat with a small ritual:
  - Revisiting the initial intentions for the retreat. What unfolded?
  - Gratitude for this wonderful moment.
  - Commitment to keep the peace for as long as possible.
  - Commitment to the next retreat.

A Two-Day Retreat

This retreat format fits well into a weekend. I like starting retreats in the evening and finishing in the afternoon. It allows for a progressive reentry at a time of day when things quiet down.

A two-day retreat is wonderful to explore in depth any of the themes discussed in the second part of this book.

Longer retreats call for a comfortable place where solitude and silence can be undisturbed. An inspiring space allows us to establish connection to the spirit. Places in or near nature work best.

LATE AFTERNOON

5 p.m.–7 p.m.

- Settling down.
- Checking all logistics, transportation, food, and drinks for the retreat. You want to start the retreat with a mind that is unencumbered by the details of everyday life.
- Marking the beginning of the retreat with a small ritual:
    - Disconnecting devices.
    - Setting an intention for the retreat.
    - Reading about the themes that you want to reflect on during this retreat.

- ○ Lighting a candle.
- ○ Making a commitment to silence, mindfulness, and seeking clarity and peace.
- Taking a moment to bask in the uninterrupted time that stretches in front of you. Suddenly, there are no deadlines, no clock, no rush, no appointments. You can just follow your natural inclinations and take your time with everything. Time opens in front of you.
- Reading, reflecting, and journaling.

EVENING
7 p.m.–9 p.m.

- Mindful silent dinner.
- Mindful shower.
- Meditation or reading.

FIRST THING IN THE MORNING

- Meditation and yoga.
- Mindful shower.
- Light breakfast.
- Journaling on the chosen theme.

MID-MORNING
10 a.m.–12 p.m.

- Long walk in nature.

MIDDAY

- Preparing lunch, eating, cleaning.
- Nap.

MID-AFTERNOON

3 p.m.–6 p.m.

- Reading, studying, and reflecting on the chosen theme.
- Following inspiration.
- Daydreaming.
- Creative activities.
- Playing.

EARLY EVENING

6 p.m.–7 p.m.

- Connecting with nature.
- Meditating.

EVENING

7 p.m.–9 p.m.

- Mindful silent dinner.
- Mindful shower.
- Meditation or reading.

FIRST THING IN THE MORNING

7 a.m.–10 a.m.

- Meditation and yoga.

- Mindful shower.
- Light breakfast.
- Journaling on the chosen theme.

MID-MORNING

10 a.m.–12 p.m.

- Long walk in nature.

MIDDAY

- Preparing lunch, eating, cleaning.
- Nap.

MID-AFTERNOON

3 p.m.–5 p.m.

- Reading, studying, and reflecting on the chosen theme.
- Following inspiration.
- Doing nothing.
- Playing.
- Creative activities.

BEFORE CLOSING THE RETREAT

- Journaling on the chosen theme and on the retreat experience.
- Marking the end of the retreat with a small ritual:
  - Revisiting the initial intentions for the retreat. What unfolded?

- Gratitude for this wonderful moment.
- Commitment to keep the peace for as long as possible.
- Commitment to the next retreat.

Longer Retreats

A longer retreat can follow the general format described above. If you can afford to carve out a week or more, many options become possible. As you settle into silence and solitude, it becomes easier to take a fresh perspective on many of your professional and personal challenges.

Over time, the small daily worries appear insignificant, and you can focus on what truly matters. Regardless of the format and location you choose, I recommend sticking to a daily structure so you don't fall into complacency or waste your precious retreat time. Decide on a routine and stick to it. Discipline creates freedom—in life as well as retreats!

RE-ENTRY

Finally, it's important that you allow for gradual re-entry into the world. After a three-week yoga retreat in a small, isolated village on the north coast of Bali, I was stunned when my wife picked me up and booked us in a nice hotel in the island's main tourist center. Even though I was overjoyed to be with her again, it took me a couple of days to process the buzz, tourists, and music. Returning to the "real world" after a retreat can sometimes be a shock.

The longer the retreat, the more you will need a buffer between the retreat and going back to your full-on life. Block a day or two, once home, to ease back into your regular rhythm. Use the time to catch up with emails or review your upcoming schedule. Save some time for silence and use your journal to write down your impressions.

ADDITIONAL JOURNALING
AND REFLECTIONS

As you reflect on the possibility of going on a retreat, you can ask yourself the following questions:

- What are my fears?
- What parts of me are resisting the idea of a retreat?
- What am I searching for?
- What am I hoping to take from my first retreat?
- What am I hoping to let go of?
- How am I taking care of myself these days?
- How would I describe the peace I desire? When was the last time I felt at peace?

PART II

CONTEMPLATIVE
LEADERSHIP

As we have seen, leaders must confront near-term business priorities while they look ahead toward shaping the world of tomorrow. Their Doing has major repercussions. Their actions can pave the way to greater equality, a supportive culture, and environmental sustainability, for example.

The challenges ahead are daunting. If there were obvious solutions to global issues, we would have found them a long time ago. Contemplative leaders understand these challenges, but their focus goes beyond the pursuit of career success, recognition, or material gains. These are often the wonderful outcomes of hard work. But even more importantly, leaders dedicate themselves to activities that fulfill their sense of purpose and have a positive impact on others. They act in such a way as to leave the world in a better shape than they found it.

Rather than set an impossible bar for themselves, contemplative leaders ask key questions: *How can I do what is best for the collective? Am I bringing my best self to every situation I encounter, no matter how trivial? When I interact with a customer, launch a product, hire new staff, or terminate a supplier, am I confident I've tackled the situation in a way that is compatible with my values?*

The essence of contemplative leadership is to develop clarity, calm, and a sense of purpose. To achieve these objectives, you can return to regular retreat time in your busy schedule. As we've seen, these retreats—taken in solitude and silence, in a conducive space—allow you to connect with your spirit.

The second part of this book explores key themes (and questions) you can explore deeply during a retreat. These themes bridge leadership and contemplation—our Doing and Being. Remember that these forces are not antagonistic, fighting to dominate us. Instead, they complement each other so we can bring the gift of our best leadership to the world.

Over the years, in conversations with hundreds of business leaders around the world, the seven themes I introduce in the following chapters have come up again and again. Each theme challenges conventional wisdom and leadership ethos. To each question, you must find your own answers. In the intimacy of deeper inquiry and exploration of the soul, there are no ready-made solutions. As a contemplative guide, I have many questions for you and very few answers.

Each chapter is structured in a similar manner. I will present a theme and share some insights drawn from different fields—management, philosophy, psychology, or spirituality. Then, I offer a few contemplations to allow you to absorb and integrate these perspectives to seek your own answers. Finally, I will conclude each chapter with a few additional journaling and reflection prompts. In the appendix, I share some inspirational books connected to each theme.

I recommend exploring the seven themes in sequence. Imagine starting a walk through a plain before reaching the hills and finally scaling the summit. You can also stay with a theme over several retreats. As the Greek philosopher Heraclitus said, "No man ever steps in the same river twice, for it's not the same river and he's not the same man." Each time you return, you will discover aspects of yourself you had not noticed.

Chapter 6

MAPPING *the*
JOURNEY

L EADERSHIP IS MADE OF SHORT AND LONG CYCLES.
Leaders must address short-term issues and take stock of
the present while they also envision an inspiring future and plan
how to get there.

At the age of forty-two, I made a significant career transition.
I realized that my dream of becoming a bank CEO was no longer
speaking to my heart. This was a devastating realization, and the
collapse of a dream that had filled me with energy for a decade and
a half. Even worse, I had no idea what to do to replace this failed
dream. It took me a good year to cross that desert, during which
I explored what my motivations were, where I was in life, and the
destination I wanted to reach in the second phase of my career.

I learned from this difficult transition and reflected on similar difficulties my clients face. As leaders, we struggle in our journeys for three reasons: we fail to identify what really motivates us, we lack a proper map to chart the journey, and we confuse journey and destination. In this chapter, I will break down each of these terms, so they are clear and distinct. Then I will share a set of contemplations designed to improve your clarity and focus.

MOTIVATION

Early in our adult life, our goals fall in the category of extrinsic motivators. As we establish ourselves in society, we must acquire status and gain recognized experience. We earn sufficient income to pay off student loans, get a house, build a family, and raise kids. I remember comparing the job offers I received when I graduated and being tempted to choose one company over another because of a few hundred dollars in salary. Even ethics-conscious millennials, who want to work for a company with a purpose, must often prioritize salary when they're just beginning in their career paths.

But even if we go after a higher salary, external rewards can only go so far. Psychologists like Edward Deci and Dan Ariely studied what motivates us to perform certain tasks. They wondered whether increasing external rewards, such as monetary incentives, makes us perform better. They found people do not necessarily perform at their best simply because they are paid well. Instead, people generally perform at their best when they derive intrinsic satisfaction from performing the activities themselves. And this makes sense, right? We all want to feel that we are competent, in control, and purposeful.

If you pursue extrinsic motivators like wealth, status, and power, without enjoying the activities that lead to these results, you won't feel inner satisfaction. The sense of joy and fulfillment comes from competently performing meaningful actions, of your own volition.

I am not advocating giving up material rewards. They come as natural consequence for your hard and competent work. And as in all hierarchies, whether human or animal, status does have its place; it can, for example, provide you with better food and increased opportunities for finding a mate. When you only seek external validation, however, you risk embarking on an endless chase. Your internal emptiness can never be filled. This is why billionaires might continue amassing wealth and expanding their empires without ever feeling truly fulfilled.

At some point, when you have your material needs met, the quest for yet more external validation—a more senior role, better pay, another house—loses meaning, leaving you empty and restless. You will never get enough of what you don't really need.

In contrast, intrinsic motivators create an inner sense of fulfillment because they align with what gives us satisfaction and meaning in life. They satisfy us year after year.

The distinction is not always obvious. The same goal, such as coaching the kids' soccer team, can provide intrinsic satisfaction to someone passionate about sports who loves being around children, or extrinsic reward for someone seeking social recognition from the community. The distinction can also reveal why turning a hobby into a job is not always a good idea. If you have to earn a living from something that gives you intrinsic satisfaction, that thing can lose the life it once had.

External motivators drove me for the first half of my career. I attended prestigious schools like INSEAD and achieved status by working as a partner at McKinsey. It was pleasant to be recognized and acknowledged. The business card opened all the doors, and I met with powerful CEOs and business owners daily.

After leaving McKinsey, I worked for another organization that gave me a similarly prestigious position. After a while, it became clear that the role was not a great fit; I hated the culture of the company. I had to make a difficult choice. I could stay and enjoy the perks and prestige of the role, or I could leave, and jump into the unknown. A new occupation would satisfy my heart and give me the freedom that I craved.

For months, I agonized over the decision. I worried about money. Would I be able to find another role? Would I end up destitute? These exaggerated concerns went through my mind over and over. It was only when I reflected on what was important to me—freedom and meaningful connections—that I could make the decision to change careers. No more banking for me.

I could use the lessons of my painful career transition and put myself at the service of others.

I see this same inner debate with my clients. Some are chasing the external reward, while others have found intrinsic meaning in what they do. An acquaintance of mine, Noah, started his own internet company, not because he cared much about the topic—a medical application—but because of the prospect of getting rich quickly. In contrast, Eric, an investor in the tech industry, loves his job. He enjoys listening to pitches, advising young founders, sharing his experience, and occasionally investing in their businesses. His passion wins him business. Despite the stress and the setbacks, he's never considered doing anything else.

Our first contemplation will help you see what motivates you to initiate a journey.

THE INTEGRAL MAP

To plan well, we need a map that allows us to grasp the complexity of human experience. We tend to oversimplify and adopt a partial viewpoint. But an experience can be seen from multiple perspectives, all of them shedding a specific light. If I am complaining from being tired and demotivated, a psychologist will seek to understand my emotions and diagnose depression whereas a general practitioner will run a blood test and recommend vitamins. My boss might take me off a project, whereas my friends will throw a party for me. Who's right and who's wrong? Each of them sees the world from a different corner of the human experience.

Similarly, to orient yourself in the complexity of your human world, you need a good map that encapsulates life's many dimensions. Understanding your starting point and how to reach your destination often necessitates acting across multiple domains. Training for a marathon is not just about physical conditioning. You need your psychological state in top shape and a support network of coaches and other runners. You need running trails for training and organized races to participate in.

An integral map allows you to appreciate the multiple dimensions of taking stock, setting goals, and preparing for the journey. When you have this, you reach clarity in all aspects of leadership and life.

Our second contemplation will show you how to build a map of the journey.

THE JOURNEY AND THE DESTINATION

I once took a group of retreat participants to a monastery in Central Java, Indonesia. Sitting in the magical, dimly lit atmosphere of this small temple, a young monk welcomed us and gave us incredibly helpful insight into the *journey* of meditation. "Meditation," he said, "is like taking a road trip. If you constantly think about reaching your destination, like Donkey asking Shrek 'Are we there yet?', you will be restless and soon give up. But if you enjoy every tiny moment of the meditation by being curious about your breath, physical sensations, and the appearance of thoughts, thirty minutes will pass by quickly."

The last issue with planning is that we spend too much time arguing about the destination and too little wondering about the journey. Lao Tzu famously said, "A journey of a thousand miles starts with a first step." After this first step comes second and third ones. You cannot lose sight of every step that will be necessary before you can reach your goal. It is one thing to imagine myself with a great beach body; it is another to go to the gym every day at 6:00 a.m. and cut out the pizza and beer.

To reach your destination, you need to have systems and routines that will carry you through the journey. If you want to finish a marathon, you'll need to create a set of habits that supports your training. No matter how inspired you are at the thought of crossing that finish line and getting a finisher T-shirt, every step toward the objective must carry its own reward.

Our last contemplation will help you reflect on the differences between journey and destination.

CONTEMPLATION 1: MOTIVATION

We have seen that there are two types of motivations—extrinsic and intrinsic. The source of extrinsic motivation comes from outside. It is given to us. It might be power, money, status and titles, fame, or belonging to a prestigious organization where we shine by association. Extrinsic motivators can easily be taken from you. You can be fired, ostracized, canceled, or demoted.

Intrinsic satisfaction comes from within. It might come from the pleasure of learning, helping others, being generous, or a job well done. Intrinsic motivators, because they are self-generated, are very hard to lose.

Relying on extrinsic motivators for your self-esteem makes you fragile and anxious. Having a solid foundation of intrinsic motivators makes you resilient.

For this first contemplation, set aside a couple of hours to review each major professional choice you've made so far. Identify the factors that motivated you toward these choices. Organize extrinsic and intrinsic motivators. Here is a useful test for distinguishing between the two: if you did not get the external reward from the work, would you still enjoy doing the work?

As you reflect, ask the following questions and see what comes up:

- What patterns do I see?
- What decisions have I made that satisfied external motivators? Internal motivators? What were the results of each set of decisions?
- What risks do I foresee when I only satisfy my extrinsic motivators? My intrinsic motivators?
- How satisfied am I about the balance between extrinsic and intrinsic motivators?

- What truly moves me?
- What steps could I take to derive more intrinsic and less extrinsic satisfaction?

CONTEMPLATION 2:
AN INTEGRAL MAP

This second contemplation is a reflection on your journey. Where are you and where are you going? In the eighties, philosopher Ken Wilber developed a framework to map our human experience comprehensively. He noticed that many disciplines were approaching our experience from different angles, but each would only see a partial picture. Wilber set to integrate all these theories into one, which he called integral.

Our experience is both subjective and objective, individual and collective. The integral framework is an elegant way of capturing all these facets simultaneously. The diagram on the following page summarizes the integral map and is adapted from the work of Ken Wilber and James Flaherty.

Organizations and leaders tend to focus on Domain 4, the tangible collective. They create organizational charts, systems, processes, and key performance indicators. Numbers don't lie, we tell ourselves. We track every possible quantitative indicator that creates a false sense of certainty, as if we know what is happening. We let go of those who don't meet targets. We shut down or sell unprofitable operations.

	SUBJECTIVE	OBJECTIVE
INDIVIDUAL	**Domain 1: Thoughts, hopes, and fears** *This is the domain of my inner world. I alone know what is going on here.* • What do I believe? • How am I feeling? What is my physical and emotional state? My mood? What are my patterns of thoughts? • What am I feeling? What is my physical state? • What am I concerned about? • What am I committed to? • What is my ambition? What do I want? • What am I experiencing? In what way am I suffering?	**Domain 2: Physical aspects and behavior** *This is what is visible of me by external observers. It is connected to my Individual Subjective quadrant, but what I think and how I behave can be very different. My thoughts and my actions may or may not be coherent.* • What is my profession? What am I doing? What am I able to do? • What is the condition of my body? • What are my behavioral habits? • How am I taking care of myself (e.g., nutrition, exercise, sleep)?
COLLECTIVE	**Domain 3: Culture and relationships** *This domain describes me as a member of the communities and cultures to which I belong.* • What is my cultural frame of reference? • What are our collective values? Our ethics? How do these influence how I interpret the world? • What roles do I play? • Who is guiding me, who is supporting me? • Who influences me? Who loves me? • Who am I in a relationship with? Who are my colleagues, my clients, my subordinates?	**Domain 4: Environment and systems** *This quadrant deals with the objective world in which I live.* • Where am I? What are the possibilities and the limitations of this place? • What resources, including financial, do I have to move in the world? • What systems do I use? How do I measure progress? • What structures my environment: laws, organization, rules, systems, processes? • What is my relationship with technology? In what way does technology serve me—or is it the other way around? • What is my relationship with nature? With my environment? How do I care for or harm my environment?

But the integral map shows that we miss three-quarters of the picture when we obsess over Domain 4. In doing so, we disregard our psyche (Domain 1), the physiological impact of our life rhythm (Domain 2), and the culture and behaviors we inhabit (Domain 3).

The response of many governments to the COVID pandemic illustrates this tunnel vision. Governments initially focused on the key metric of virus spread (Domain 4) to design policies of social distancing. They ignored the impact of those decisions on people's ability to exercise (Domain 2) and meet their friends and families (Domain 3). They overlooked the impact of isolation on students and the elderly. Mental health issues crept up (Domain 1). We may have saved lives, but the impact of restrictive policies will be felt for years.

The four quadrants are mutually exclusive—one cannot be reduced or included in another. They are also collectively exhaustive—they capture our entire experience. Why is this relevant to leadership and contemplation? Because stillness helps you comprehend the full impact of your actions. Through contemplation, you can plan the journey ahead without tunnel vision.

For this reflection, take a couple of hours and draw your own map on a sheet of paper.

To illustrate, here is an example from Sergio, the airline CEO I guided through this reflection. Sergio had recently retired from a powerful position. In our conversations, he was feeling defeated and without purpose, invisible and unimportant, even though he was well regarded in his industry and frequently sought after for advice. At this point in time, he occupied several nonexecutive roles that kept him busy and well compensated. The following page shows what came out of his first reflection.

From this table, Sergio learned that Domain 3 was a powerful energy source to help him drive changes in Domains 1 and 2. The support from his family and his sense of commitment allowed him to embark on a fitness drive. He lost 40 pounds in six months. At the same time, he and I worked on resolving Domain 1 topics, such as finding professional meaning as a young retiree.

Now it's your turn. Fill in your integral map and see what comes up.

CONTEMPLATION 3:
THE JOURNEY AND THE DESTINATION

The previous reflection focused on the present. Only a deep and dispassionate examination of the present can reveal the journey you must undertake. In this third contemplation, you will reflect on the journey more than on the destination. You must ensure that you enjoy every step to complete your thousand-mile journey. At the heart of the journey are the routines you want to create.

Analyze the map you created in the previous contemplation. How would you adjust your present situation? What are the habits that you need to create to fulfill every quadrant? How will you spend your time on each domain?

Sergio's Integral Map: Starting Point

SUBJECTIVE	OBJECTIVE
Domain 1: Thoughts, hopes, and fears	**Domain 2: Physical aspects and behavior**
• I am not happy. I feel that what I am doing currently is not fulfilling. • I am open to a new way of thinking. • I don't feel I am having an impact. • I am excited about the next phase of my life. • I am disciplined and prepared to do what it takes. • I value hard work, status, and success.	• I want to get in good physical shape. • I don't exercise enough and lack energy. • I have a strong physical presence.
Domain 3: Culture and relationships	**Domain 4: Environment and systems**
• I am close to my family. They will support me on this journey. • I am fundamentally a capitalist, and I believe in markets and individual enterprise. No one will rescue me, and I must put in the work. • That said, I can also take advantage of extensive networks in the industry.	• I am measured in the world by how much I make. • I want to downsize my life. I don't need such a big house now that my kids are independent. • I rely heavily on technology for news and communications. I am constantly connected.

(INDIVIDUAL — rows 1–2; COLLECTIVE — rows 3–4)

To help Sergio reflect, I encouraged him to spend time on retreats. He had never spent time on his own during his career. As a senior executive, he was always accompanied by colleagues on his travels. We first designed short retreats, which he progressively extended. In the end, Sergio regularly spent several days on his own to complete his reflections.

His journey covered all four quadrants. He started on Domain 2 to get energy from a radical physical transformation based on regular exercise and better nutrition. In Domain 3, he cut toxic relationships. He became selective about the businesses and individuals he engaged with and the appointments he accepted. This allowed him to invest more time with his friends and family. Our work on Domain 1 created confidence and clarity about who he really was and what he could bring to the world. Lastly, in Domain 4, Sergio proceeded to simplify his life. He sold vacation homes he did not need anymore and moved into a smaller house. He also spent more time on his own in a place dear to his heart in Italy.

As you examine your own integral map, see what stands out. Are the four domains balancing each other or are they out of sync? Which domains appear strong? Which appear weak? What is the journey that starts emerging in front of you?

SUMMARY

As you embark on any project, professional transformation, or life journey, contemplate on:

- Your motivation for the journey—extrinsic or intrinsic.
- The integral map of your present position and of the journey—comprehensively exploring all the quadrants of the human experience.
- A distinction between the journey and the destination and getting clarity on the individual steps required across all domains to reach your destination.

This set of contemplations is ideal for short retreats. As you take time to reflect, you will experience a new sense of calm, balance, and clarity.

ADDITIONAL JOURNALING
AND REFLECTIONS

- What is the narrative that underpins my planning? Am I falling prey to standard narratives among modern-day leaders, such as:
  - Am I overly focused on performance? What is the metric that I am pursuing to measure my success in life?
  - Do I want to improve myself because I feel deficient or insufficient in some way? Am I seeking to improve the way the world sees me? Am I feeling that I am not enough, and I should do more of something?

- ○ Am I expecting that when I accomplish one of my key goals, my life will suddenly be good?
- In what way are these narratives helpful or harmful?
- What parts of my self-image am I attached to? What roles am I attached to? Is this attachment still useful today, or could I let it go?

Chapter 7

CULTIVATING PRESENCE

BOUT A DECADE AGO, I FACED ANOTHER DIFFICULT choice: should I stay at my prestigious executive search firm even though the environment was toxic? Or should I leave and start my own practice? I listened attentively and heard three inner voices: Mr. Freedom encouraged me to move on ("You can do so much better without all these politics."). Mr. Anxious worried about how I would make a living. And Mr. Status wondered whether clients would still work with me if I did not carry a recognized brand name.

In their own way, these voices wanted the best for me. Mr. Freedom wanted to protect me from the toxicity of the environment. Mr. Anxious did not want me to get in financial trouble. Mr. Status wanted me to be recognized.

One by one, I addressed my inner friends with gratitude and appreciation. "Thank you for your concern," I said to each. I made them feel seen, valued, and understood. They relaxed progressively, and I felt this physical release. The tension and the noise went away. I now found serenity and strength. Whatever I chose to do, I knew that I would be okay. I decided to leave. The road ahead was challenging, but I never regretted it. Immense personal growth followed, giving me opportunities I never would have had otherwise.

When you cultivate self-awareness and cut through the layers of narratives and inner voices, you can connect with your deepest qualities. These qualities reside at the core of your consciousness, hard to notice because of the external noise.

Why should you even bother? Self-awareness and discovering how you show up in the world are not part of the mainstream curriculum in business school. Leadership training focuses on organizing, influencing, motivating, negotiating, selling, and communicating. But surprisingly little is taught about knowing ourselves.

For leaders, self-inquiry is not on their top priority list. The topic provokes reactions of rejection ("I am not crazy." or "There is nothing wrong with me."), surprise ("What could I learn that I don't already know?"), or dismissal ("It's a nice idea, but let's be realistic here: I have a business to run."). A little deeper down, there may also be the fear that we might learn something we don't like about ourselves ("Let sleeping dogs lie.").

Not surprisingly, you don't know yourself as well as you think you do. The first step in this quest for self-awareness is spending time alone or in the company of a guide—a therapist, coach, mentor, spiritual advisor. Here, you can explore the layers of your consciousness and get to the source of your very being.

Cultivating self-awareness is an important driver of personal and professional growth. It allows you to understand your views, the decisions you make, and how you act. This prevents you from going too far down the wrong road.

Self-awareness also allows you to understand and address your cognitive biases. You become aware of your tendencies to be too optimistic, confident, or cautious. Over time, you make better decisions.

An inner inquiry may also reveal deeper behavioral patterns that developed at a very young age. Children behave to secure parental love and, in some cases, avoid punishment or abuse. These deeply ingrained patterns were critical for survival but likely become outdated after thirty, forty, or fifty years. Yet, they remain active, to protect us from hurt and a threat that has long disappeared.

WHY PRESENCE MATTERS

Two major emotional intelligence qualities drive your personal growth. The first, self-awareness, is a direct consequence of presence. We will explore the second, interpersonal skills, in the next chapter on relationships.

Self-awareness connects you to your emotions and feelings, and gives you the capacity to respond skillfully. It is an important marker of personal growth. By inserting a space between stimulus and response, you develop freedom. For example, you become free not to be deflated by a client's negative answer. You develop a deeper sense of your inner world and become capable of looking within and understanding what is going on. What emotions are you experiencing and what causes them? More importantly, how do you develop a skillful response?

Your emotional responses are tested every day. Deliverables do not meet your standards. You miss deadlines. Promises are broken and contracts are renegotiated. All of this may take place when you are tired or anxious. You risk letting your emotional responses overwhelm you.

Self-awareness is neither taught nor encouraged in school or university or the workplace. Instead, the prevailing culture focuses on building or simulating confidence. We are influenced by charismatic figures like Steve Jobs or Jack Welch. We are Cartesians at heart, and we persist in separating our thoughts from our emotions.

We know now, thanks to advances in neurosciences, that we cannot dissociate mind from body. Your body is not a device only designed to carry your brain from one place to another. In fact, the more you reject your physical sensations, emotions, and feelings, the narrower your thinking becomes.

When you develop presence, you wake up to your life. If you operate on autopilot with your attention scattered between past and future, you cannot anchor yourself in the present moment. Yet, this is the only moment that will ever exist. Everything else is fantasy. This is a fundamental teaching in all the contemplative traditions.

Presence means engaging with situations with your full attention, without being carried away by your own narratives and the various characters that live in your head. You can bring your whole self to the situation. When you listen, you listen. When you write an email, you write an email. You bring your full intellectual, emotional, and physical capacity. All your senses are engaged. In a world of distraction, short attention span, polarization, five-minute meetings, and constant interruptions, leaders with presence are profoundly reassuring.

PEELING THE LAYERS OF CONSCIOUSNESS

Who am I? Sages have mulled over this simple question since human consciousness began. The classic spiritual literature in the East is in no small part devoted to this question. In the West, we often answer with superficial labels. These include gender, nationality, race, profession, relationship status, sexual orientation, the causes we love, political orientation, or defining life events. I am male, American, Asian, a financial advisor, divorced, heterosexual, a marathon runner, a democrat, and a cancer survivor.

All these labels are transient and artificial. No matter how real they seem, they only correspond to a narrative that you repeat to yourself thousands of times until you believe it. But in the end, you know no more about yourself than when you started.

You are made of layers. The most superficial layer is your *physical body*. It determines your appearance and belonging to some of the labels described earlier. This external layer is, of course, what you notice first about someone. Often, it is the basis for assumptions and judgments.

One level deeper, you uncover a thick and sticky mush of *narratives and beliefs that drive your behaviors*. There is a whole cast of characters, each with their own mission and agenda. You may be aware of some. Yet many are below the surface, and it takes some proactive exploration to uncover them.

Here are some vignettes that illustrate these narratives. Salman gets angry when his boss challenges him. Yet, he is prompt to admit that his boss makes very smart remarks. What triggers Salman is not so much the challenge as the feeling of inadequacy; he should have thought about it before the boss. Where does this trigger come from? What deeper part of him feels inadequate or threatened and provokes anger as a protective reaction?

Enrique feels like an impostor. He was appointed to the executive committee of a global industrial corporation at the age of thirty-six and felt that he was not ready for this promotion. The feeling did not leave Enrique in the last fifteen years despite continued success. What hides behind this narrative that he is not good enough for the role?

Tina tends to withdraw when facing conflict. She is a competent, analytical, and highly regarded supply chain leader. But she
lacks assertiveness. When colleagues disagree with her, she shuts
down and withdraws. What triggers her to do so? In our conversations, she realized that this reactive mechanism developed
in her youth. It is a protection against the hurt that may result
from disagreements.

Chris has difficulty showing his emotions, even to his wife,
whom he adores. He is well known in the marketing industry
as a guide to the younger generation. He was recently featured
on the cover of a trade magazine as one of the guiding lights of
the profession. He was deeply touched but at a loss about how
to react. Should he show joy? Any expression of emotion seems
fake to him. He will eventually be able to link his discomfort
with emotional displays to his childhood. His abusive father
punished him whenever he cried or showed happiness. Showing
an emotion was a risk for young Chris. Today, this outdated
software is still guiding his behaviors.

Salman, Enrique, Tina, and Chris all have these inner characters who react to external events and drive their behaviors.

We erect protective barriers to avoid being hurt. They are the
legacy of our childhood when we were defenseless and had to
devise strategies to be loved by our caregivers. Time and again,
we were wounded, even when we were raised in loving families. Over time, we created these protective mechanisms that
progressively solidified. For many, these childhood wounds are

minor. For some, they are much deeper and the result of physical or emotional abuse. When we become familiar with this layer of protective parts, we can finally understand our behaviors.

Let's continue our descent. One level deeper, we finally reach *the field of consciousness*—clear and spacious as the sky. It has no beginning and no end. Thoughts, feelings, physical sensations, emotions, memories, and intentions are projected into this field. They are like clouds in this infinite sky. They are transient and come and go.

Buddhist nun Pema Chodron says: "You are the sky. Everything else is just the weather." Sometimes, your mind is busy, cluttered, agitated; the sky is overcast, and nothing shines through. Other times, you are calm, relaxed, and open; the clouds are few and far between. In those moments, you can take the measure of the eternal presence of your consciousness. This is your deepest essence.

It is at this deep level that your essential qualities of presence reside. At your core, you find peace, generosity, stability, compassion, joy, love, strength, and patience. If you cut through the layers of physical appearance, narratives, and protective and reactive parts, you access these essential qualities and let them shine through you. However, the various protective layers are thick. And the flow of essential qualities is often blocked from emerging and shining. Your qualities remain buried deep inside you.

Getting to know yourself through the examination of these various layers takes time and practice. It never happens in the midst of the noise and agitation of your daily life. But in stillness and silence, and often with the help of a guide, you can access the essence of your spirit. This is presence at work.

HOW TO ACCESS PRESENCE

The best way to access presence is to slow down and examine the narrative, various characters, and inner voices that are active below the surface. When you sit in stillness, you can notice which parts are acting up. Perhaps you feel anxious about a potential confrontation with a colleague. Or you can't stop working crazy hours even though you know you should spend more time with your family. Or you can't stop criticizing yourself.

Give names to the characters that come up. Mr. Angry is a frequent visitor of mine. Mr. Angry shows up when I feel misunderstood or treated unfairly. He expresses himself by making my body tense, raising my voice, and using sarcasm. I can trace this all the way back to when I skipped a year ahead in school when I was a kid. Everyone around me was one or two years older. Mr. Angry emerged to protect me.

Instead of chasing him away, I engaged Mr. Angry in a dialogue. What is your job? What are you protecting me from? I also appreciated Mr. Angry for all the hard work he had put in to protect me over the years. This resulted in Mr. Angry feeling appreciated. Over time, he softened up and gave me enough space to create new behaviors to resolve conflict.

It is only when you value and understand your inner characters that you can slowly move beyond them. Here, you open the door to a quiet space where your best qualities can blossom. The feeling is like diving into the sea. There may be wind, rain, and waves crashing on the surface. But as you go deeper and deeper, you find a place of peace and stillness.

The following contemplations will guide you to develop presence. The first four are introductory practices to slow the mind and develop greater awareness. The last two take you deeper, first into your emotions and finally into the characters or inner voices that populate your subconscious.

CONTEMPLATION 1:
MEDITATION ON THE BREATH

This is the core pillar of meditation. You sit still in a comfortable position and strive to remain aware of the breath, wherever you can notice it best. It may be at the tip of the nose, in the chest, or in the belly.

Sit with your back straight. Place your awareness at the breath. When thoughts arise, let them vanish and don't follow them. This is much easier said than done, and you will get distracted. A thought, noise, physical sensation, and off you go, following a random train of thought. As soon as you notice that you have drifted away, return to the breath. Don't beat yourself up. Don't judge. It's okay!

With practice, you will notice how thoughts arise at random. You are never in control of what thought will come next. This is a fundamental realization that runs counter to the belief that we are in charge of our minds.

A timer is helpful. It is good to start with short, two-minute practices and progressively extend to twenty minutes.

The breath is your most important anchor and support to developing presence. It is always available to you. Reconnecting with your breath at critical moments of the day is a gateway to presence. It allows you to shift your focus from the outside world to your inner world.

CONTEMPLATION 2:
SIMPLE MIND-BODY-HEART CHECK-IN

This practice takes only a few moments. It can be inserted at any point during the day when you feel a need to center yourself, like before starting a conversation or jumping into a new activity.

Sit in your chair with your back straight. Imagine that a thread is attached to the crown of your head, pulling toward the sky, stretching the spine. Place your feet flat on the floor. Rest your hands into your lap in a way that allows you to relax arms and shoulders.

Read the following instructions first, and then practice.

Let your eyes close softly. Take three deep and slow breaths. Bring your body to stillness. A stable body is a prerequisite to a stable mind.

- First, bring your awareness to your mind. What is going on in your head? What are you preoccupied with? What are your worries, your hopes? What is on your to-do list?

- Second, bring your awareness to your body. What physical sensations do you notice? Are you energized, calm, or tired? Scan from toe to head and notice the points of contact between your body and the floor, the chair, your clothes, the movement of the air in the room against your skin, the expansion of the chest and belly with the breath. Follow your curiosity.

- Third, bring your awareness to your heart. How are you feeling today? Happy, anxious, frustrated, optimistic? What emotions can you notice and name? If you are not used to naming emotions, start with the easy ones and progressively expand your emotional vocabulary. If you are having difficulties describing your emotions, go to Contemplation 5 and use the emotions map that I have prepared for you.

This check-in is one of the simplest practices of contemplative leadership. It invites you to consider the question: "What is going on with me?"

You can repeat this check-in several times a day: when you wake up, before a meeting, or at the end of the day. You can even set a timer on your phone to chime every hour, and perform a thirty-second version of the practice.

CONTEMPLATION 3:
OPEN AWARENESS MEDITATION

In open awareness meditation, we first focus on the breath. Then, we expand our field of awareness and include other objects, such as physical sensations, sounds, thoughts, and emotions.

As always, we are observers of what is. We observe without judgment or reaction. We maintain an attitude of nonreactive curiosity to anything that arises in our lives.

First, place your awareness on the breath and stay there a few minutes.

Next, become aware of physical sensations. Notice what arises and whether the sensation is pleasurable, neutral, or unpleasant. Notice how these sensations are fleeting; your body is constantly in a state of flow. With practice, you can perceive the qualities of this flow: warm or cold, dense or hollow, dark or light, steady or moving or pulsating, organized or erratic, expanding or contracting.

You can also notice the movement of the air and the texture of your clothes on the skin. You feel the expansion and contraction of your chest and abdomen when you breathe. You are lifted by the upward push of the floor against your feet and the chair against your buttocks.

Feelings and emotions may also arise. They first materialize as physical sensations: tense muscles, a clenched jaw, butterflies in the belly, warmth on our face and throat, or a void in our chest. The tension that you carry in your body reflects your emotional state, expressed or suppressed. You can explore, inquire, and relax. Sometimes, a self-massage helps ease the residual tension.

Next, bring your awareness to sounds. We rarely notice how rich our environment is. If you are in a city, there will be traffic and honking and construction. Buildings have their own sounds, too: cracking, air conditioning hum, voices, music, clatter, and vibrations. In nature, it could be the wind rustling leaves, birds, distant human noises, or a stream. The complexity of our sound environment often goes unnoticed. But with full awareness, you may be able to perceive five or more distinct sources of sound.

Next, observe how your thoughts arise and vanish. With practice, you no longer get hooked to your thoughts. You are no longer compelled to jump on that train and let it take you to its random destination. You can simply notice when a thought arises and let it pass, like a cloud in the sky.

In *The Power of Now*, spiritual teacher Eckhart Tolle suggests an experiment: "Close your eyes, and say to yourself: 'I wonder what my next thought is going to be.' Then, become very alert and wait for the next thought. Be like a cat watching a mouse hole. What thought is going to come out of the mouse hole?" I encourage you to try this experiment. And each time you see a new "mouse," let it pass by and be ready for the next. Again, the task is to simply notice.

Finally, immerse yourself in this entire field of awareness. Integrate breath, physical sensations, emotions, sounds, and thoughts, and sit in the middle of everything.

CONTEMPLATION 4:
MINDFULNESS IN ACTION

We do not need to sit still to practice mindfulness. The daily activities that we normally perform on autopilot can become the object of our sustained attention.

For example:

- When you go for a walk, simply observe everything
  with an attitude of curiosity. Notice how you walk,
  the miracle of maintaining your balance as you
  alternate standing on one leg and then the other.
  Observe the colors and textures. Listen to the sounds.
  If you practice this awareness in the streets of a city,
  notice how everyone else is busy looking at their
  phones, earbuds shielding them from this moment
  of reality.

- Practice mindful eating. Bring the food to your mouth,
  and slowly feel the taste and the texture. Masticate

slowly and observe how the taste evolves. Resist the urge to prepare another mouthful with your fork or spoon. To help you with that, rest your cutlery on the table while you are still chewing. Only after swallowing can you prepare the next bite.

- When you shower, don't rush to soap and washing. Take a moment to feel the water dripping on your skin. Observe the sensations on your body. Play with the hot and cold, noticing the emotions and feelings triggered by varying temperatures.

CONTEMPLATION 5:
UNDERSTANDING EMOTIONS

Few leaders are familiar with identifying and labeling emotions. In fact, the modern ethos of the corporate world requires you to repress your emotions. Describing someone as emotional is rarely a compliment. After years of this silencing and repressing, you become numb.

Your emotions reflect the full richness of what makes you human, and they are an integral part of your being. When you ignore your emotions, you ignore a wealth of information about yourself and others.

Emotions arise in response to external situations or internal thoughts. They come with physical sensations, such as tightness, expansion, warmth or cold, flowing energy, tearing, and rigidity or fluidity, and many other processes.

It is critical for leaders to attune to emotions and understand the three-way relationship between emotions, thoughts, and physical sensations. This allows you to expand self-awareness and manage and channel emotions in a much more effective way. For example, instead of reacting with anger to a colleague's email, you can pause. You notice your anger coming up. You become aware of the associated physical sensation, such as warmth in the face. By doing this, you create a space of freedom. You no longer have to respond angrily. Perhaps you can change posture and take a few breaths instead. You can give your colleague the benefit of the doubt. You can assume positive intent. Finally, you can type your response with a calm mind.

Key to this exploration is expanding your emotional vocabulary. Many senior executives have a limited way of describing what they feel. This is understandable given our lack of training and the systematic repression of emotions at school and the workplace. A dictionary of emotions allows you to enrich your vocabulary and identify the nuances in your emotional spectrum. You can distinguish four basic emotion families: happy, sad, mad, and scared.

Sit and observe your mood. With the help of the map on the following page, notice what emotions you are experiencing. Repeat this at various times during the day.

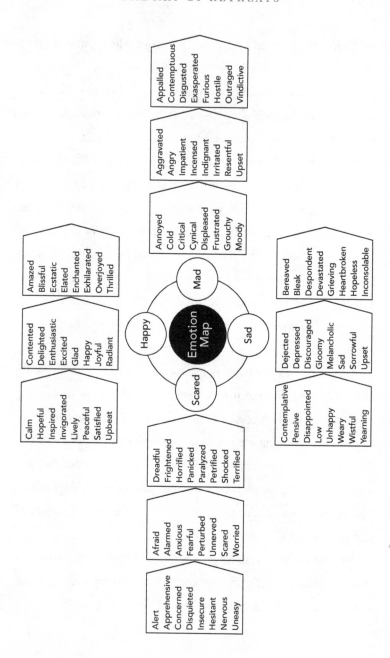

CONTEMPLATION 6:
WORKING WITH INNER VOICES

This practice allows you to quickly access a state of nonjudgmental presence. Through visualization, you access the first layers of your subconscious that usually remain hidden. The practice is inspired by depth psychology and internal family systems and was introduced to me by my teacher, Steve March. As a starting point for this contemplation, visualize yourself sitting in the middle of "everything." Around you are all the people you interact with, and all the projects, activities, interrogations, hopes, and worries that keep your mind busy. Take a few deep breaths to settle down. See what comes to the forefront of your consciousness.

For example, you might be worried about a decision you need to make, or a project that you oversee. Identify the various forces at work, pulling you in different directions. These are your inner characters or "parts." What do they want? Our parts fall into several categories—critical, worried, curious, defiant—but they always tend to our best interest. Perhaps the first character you hear is your inner critic, never satisfied with what you do and always pushing you to do better. You may hear a voice that is worried about money, which wants you to be free and independent or wants to feel loved.

Select one part at a time, treat it like an independent character, and ask the following:

- Who are you?
- What is your role? What do you want for me?
- What are you worried would happen to me if you were not here?
- What do you want to tell me?

Finally, tell the inner character how much you appreciate its role and everything it does for you. Express heartfelt thanks and gratitude. This will let the character relax. You can continue the dialogue from that point on, asking the part whether it feels satisfied now or still feels compelled to do its job.

At first, you may feel weird talking to yourself. Perhaps you believe that there is no one to talk to, or that you will not hear answers. Try it for yourself. You will be surprised.

When an inner character suddenly feels seen and valued, notice the release in your heart. Notice how you can now feel in touch with your deepest qualities, such as serenity, joy, compassion, stability, or strength.

In truth, these qualities are always here with you. This is why the narratives that you tell yourself, that you are incomplete and insufficient, are fundamentally wrong. You are always whole and can access presence whenever you need to—if you know how to relax your superficial protective layers.

SUMMARY

The state of presence, which is indispensable if we want to bring your true self to the world, is achieved when you become self-aware and connect with the essential qualities that lie at the core of your consciousness.

To access presence, you must first still the mind and body. This can be done using traditional mindfulness and meditation techniques. You start by noticing thoughts and physical sensations. Then you move deeper. Many leaders struggle with noticing and describing emotions. The emotions map can act as a guide.

Finally, once the mind is still, you become aware of and engage with your inner voices. It is the appreciation—not the rejection—of these inner parts that allows you to relax and access your fundamental qualities.

ADDITIONAL JOURNALING
AND REFLECTIONS

- *Contemplation 1.* What is my resistance to looking within?

- *Contemplation 2.* What happens in me when I meditate on the breath and get bored? What happens when I gently push through the agitation and boredom to reach the other side?

- *Contemplation 3.* What did I discover during the open awareness meditation? How am I feeling physically right now? How would I describe the sensations using the vocabulary of images, colors, textures, temperatures, densities, energy, and movement?

- *Contemplation 4.* Reflecting on what happened as I practiced mindfulness: What did I discover about the world? About myself?

- *Contemplation 5.* Using the expanded emotion vocabulary map: What mood am I in right now? What is the context or the causes for this mood? If I scan my body, what physical sensations can I associate with this mood? Is the mood an intrinsic feeling, or am I interpreting physical sensations and context to determine which mood I should feel? In other words, is the mood creating the physical sensations, or are physical sensations interpreted as a mood?

- *Contemplation 6.* With what part of myself did I connect today? What made this connection possible? What becomes possible when I trust myself? What judgment do I make about myself? What are my sources of uniqueness?

- Experiment with the relationship between physical posture and mood. Adopt the following standing postures:
    - Standing rigidly at attention, with arms stiff and jaw clenched.
    - Hunching.
    - Folding arms across the chest.
    - Standing relaxed, with feet hip-width apart and arms loose.
    - Pulling the pelvis forward and swaying the body back to compensate, with hands on your hips or in your pockets.

What shifts do you observe in your mood? What do the postures evoke? What images come up?

Chapter 8

DEEPENING
RELATIONSHIPS

N O ONE CAN LIVE WITHOUT RELATIONSHIPS. THEY
allow us to survive as infants and develop into healthy
adults. We are pack animals and need others around us for our
basic needs. The tribe provides safety, food, and belonging.

Building connections is an essential aspect of leadership. There
are no leaders without followers. Leaders connect with their
board of directors, bosses, and subordinates. They build relationships with colleagues, customers, suppliers, and regulators. They
build teams, without which organizations do not function.

Building relationships requires us to find a delicate balance
between separation and fusion. This polarity is present in any
relationship, and navigating it well is the mark of a healthy adult.

In a romantic relationship, a couple must find the balance between independence and dependence. You need to claim your individuality and independence. Yet, you also want to become one with each other. In leadership, too, you need to strike equilibrium. Too close, and you lose your independence of action and thought. Too distant, and you lose connection and influence. You must set the cursor on a continuum between lone wolf and puppet.

THE GIFT OF ATTENTION

You build relationships by giving your full attention to others. I first understood the power of giving someone my full attention at a weeklong training program for aspiring partners at McKinsey. In one session, a trainer played the role of a client. One of us had to interview the "client" while the others watched. The purpose of the exercise was to understand what the client's problem was. Keen to show our intellectual prowess, we were tempted to stop asking questions and offer suggestions. Often, we interrupted the client mid-sentence.

When my turn came to interview the "client," I simply asked him, "What are you grappling with?" and shut up. After that, I maintained eye contact and remained silent. In truth, I did not have superior listening skills. I just had no idea what to say next. So I thought I might as well keep my mouth shut rather than say something stupid. After what seemed a long time but might have only been a few minutes, the trainer exclaimed, "This is amazing, I have never felt so listened to and understood in my life."

Many books explain the basics of networking and relationships. I want to move beyond tricks and consider the heart of true connection, which is at the core of contemplative leadership. We build trust and create opportunities for others to develop by giving them the gift of attention.

We all want to receive attention. We all want to feel seen and heard, understood, and appreciated. This is an important vector of personal growth. True conversations are the fertile soil in which the seeds of confidence, balance, wisdom, and compassion can germinate. You cannot develop in a relationship where you are not understood. This is true at home and at work. Someone who has never felt seen cannot know the empowerment that arises from this connection.

Leaders, more than anyone else, empower others through the quality of their attention and conversations. Again, this goes beyond tactics and tricks. It's not about paraphrasing or nodding your head. This is about bringing your full being—mind, heart, and body—into the conversation to attune to all the dimensions of this exchange. Your conversations are more than verbal. True attention goes beyond words. Movement, pauses, posture, vibrations, and breath give you important clues about the other person.

INTIMACY, POSSIBILITIES, AND ACTION

To better understand how to deepen relationships, it is useful to map the structure of conversations. Our interactions fall into three main types: building intimacy, exploring possibilities, and organizing action. Every interaction you have—sharing perspectives, gossiping at the coffee machine, agreeing on objectives and resources, negotiating, resolving conflict, giving feedback, or mentoring—falls into one of these categories.

Intimacy is the starting point of a relationship. You look for shared interests or commonalities in your backgrounds. As trust builds up, you share more. You learn to show vulnerability, too. For example, you may need to admit ignorance or apologize and find it harder than you thought. The inability to be vulnerable will always halt the deepening of a relationship, whether in business or personal life.

After you build intimacy, you start exploring possibilities. You visualize, hypothesize, and dream together. You can create a joint future together.

Finally, you organize action by agreeing on goals, approaches, and means. This leads to plans, negotiations, reviews, and feedback. You share information and make commitments. You celebrate successes and analyze failures or ignore them.

This conversation structure repeats itself in life and business. A couple meets and builds intimacy. They explore the possibility of making a life together. This turns into action—such as marriage, kids, and dual career management.

Likewise, two businesspersons meet and get to know each other. They explore the possibility of doing a deal together. Again, this may lead to action, such as negotiations and execution.

Deepening relationships relies on giving attention and entering meaningful conversations across intimacy, possibilities, and action. But several pitfalls can derail your efforts. The three major killers of relationships are interruptions, hyper-efficiency, and polarizations. Let's examine them one by one. The contemplations at the end of the chapter will guide you to eliminate them so you can deepen your connection with others.

INTERRUPTIONS

The first impediment to deepening a relationship is interruptions. When is the last time you could articulate a view without someone interrupting? And can you listen to someone with complete attention? Can you avoid thinking about your response while the person is still talking? Can you avoid asking clarifying questions until they have finished exposing their views? Can you just be with the other, holding that sacred space?

Rather than trying to understand others, we often seek to convince them. We don't let them express their ideas. We struggle with fostering a supportive environment in which their thinking can blossom. Instead, we interrupt and abort the thinking.

Most of the time, we do this without noticing, with no ill intent. Perhaps we want to show that we understand, and we finish their sentence. Or we suggest a word when they hesitate. Sometimes, we have a question and must ask it right now, as if we could not hold it until we hear the other's view. Sometimes we get impatient. We have thought about an idea and cannot wait to spurt it out. Even our supportive nods, "uh-huhs," and "okay's" can disrupt the other person's train of thought. Whatever our reasons, we are sending a message that the other person's thinking can be cut.

Interruptions are not the exception but the norm in communication today. Observe your next staff meeting and count the number of interruptions. Watch how difficult it is for someone to articulate anything without being questioned or cut off with a comment. Watch how rich thinking is stifled. We don't seek to listen for understanding; we prefer to make our own points.

Tim, the founder of a successful tech company, asked me to observe his executive committee meeting. It was unclear whether the purpose of the meeting was information sharing or problem-solving. It turned out to be neither. I sat quietly in a corner of the meeting room as fifteen senior executives took their seats around the boardroom table. One by one, these bright engineers and salespeople started presenting their updates and proposals. Each time, the founder interrupted after one minute. He had questions, comments, instructions, and challenges. These were certainly valid points, but no thinking was possible. Later, the demoralized engineers confessed that they respected Tim's intellect but did not feel heard. The worst part was that I knew Tim had only good intentions and wanted to push his people to produce their best thinking. He was, unknowingly, achieving the opposite effect. While it is the responsibility of leaders to harness the best thinking of their teams, this can hardly happen in a flow of constant interruptions.

HYPER-EFFICIENCY

Trust builds over time and over meaningful conversations. Yet fragmentation and pressure leave little room for intimacy and possibilities. You cannot give your full attention when your eyes are constantly trained on the clock. You are too busy dealing with action. You might be skilled at tactical conversations, but these leave little room for relationship building. One person is simply a means to another person's goal.

The alternative—and ethical—approach is what German philosopher Immanuel Kant called the categorical imperative: "Act in such a way that you treat humanity, whether in your own person or in the person of any other, never merely as a means, but always at the same time as an end."

Yet even the best-intentioned leaders become the victims of hurry and hyperactivity. Some promote five-minute meetings, thinking this is helpful for everyone. You'll need to make your point in less than five minutes or expect to be cut off.

Discussions are short. Topics that need more time will be deliberated "offline." Attention deficit becomes a virtue, praised in the name of efficiency.

Hyperactivity also hurts relationship building at home. We would love to spend more time with our kids but "must" check emails. We have a brief check-in with our partner but "can't" give our attention to the issue they would like to discuss. As Harvard professor Clay Christensen pointed out, when we have thirty minutes, we often allocate the time to activities that give us a sense of immediate achievements, such as responding to emails or sending a proposal to a client. We don't build relationships because these take years to blossom.

POLARIZATION AND IDEOLOGIES

To achieve meaningful conversations and deepen relationships, you must seek to understand someone else's views. When you cross that bridge, you open yourself to a world of new possibilities.

Unfortunately, true debate has all but disappeared from our culture. Politicians demolish their opponents systematically because they belong to a different camp. Social media platforms have given rise to the most vicious violence, ostracism, and "cancel culture." Search engines act as echo chambers and return the results we are likely to agree with based on our previous browsing history. Post-modern ideologies proliferate. Under the guise of tolerance and freedom of expression, we live in one of the most intolerant and controlling periods in human history.

Some ideologies turn into dogmatic beliefs, and these systems dominate the cultural space. The ideology relies on self-fulfilling confirmation bias and the rejection of contradictory debate. They do not seek to give attention and understanding but to destroy contradiction. They present a half-picture of reality, never a full picture. Reality is never as simple as ideologues would like you to believe.

Certain ideologies have led to religious fundamentalism, political beliefs such as Nazism and Marxism, and post-modern creeds such as identity politics and cultural relativism. These are all powerful belief systems. Those who subscribe to them are willing to kill for them, literally or figuratively.

The executive coach James Flaherty observes in his *Integral Coaching* course that while we recognize that other people may have different views than ours, we also believe those views are not as good as our own. We tend to dismiss them rather rapidly. According to Flaherty, "To be in a genuine or authentic conversation with someone means that we are ready and willing to hear, as from an equal, what he can tell us. Underlying this developmental leap is the profound insight that the human world is invariably constructed by interpretation."

Opening to others' views means that you enter a dialogue prepared to change your point of view. There can be several answers to the same question. Of course, not all ideas and opinions are equally valid. Some opinions are highly questionable. The point is, you can only decide after you have thoroughly tried to understand the other person.

The quality of conversation between two persons who seek to understand each other will be greatly satisfying, even if they do not converge in the end.

In the face of intolerance and dogma, I am inspired by the words of psychiatrist Scott Peck, in *The Different Drum: Community Making and Peace*. He wrote that "the overall purpose of human communication is—or should be—reconciliation. It should ultimately serve to lower or remove the walls of misunderstanding which unduly separate us human beings, one from another."

In this context, how can leaders build deep relationships? How can we make the people around us feel seen, acknowledged, and understood? The following contemplations will guide you in this direction. The first contemplation invites you to deepen your conversations and fight interruptions and hyper-efficiency. The other three contemplations deal with building equanimity and compassion, to fight intolerance and polarizations.

CONTEMPLATION 1:
DEEPENING CONVERSATIONS

In *Time to Think*, Nancy Kline writes, "The quality of your attention determines the quality of other people's thinking." In this contemplation, reflect on the conversations you want to have and how to deepen them. Are your conversations subject to the following occurrences?

- *Interruptions from outside.* For example, your phone is invited to the conversation by being placed on the table. Your attention may be diverted when a new message arrives. The same goes when you meet in a public place where you can easily be interrupted by others.

- *Interruptions from inside.* You jump in and interrupt when the other person is still talking or reflecting. You may do this because you are eager to share, you think fast, you want to signal that you have understood, your ideas are better, you're afraid you will lose your own thoughts if you don't express them immediately, you are the boss and it is okay to dominate the conversation, or you are in a rush.

- *Assumptions.* What are you assuming about this person that is limiting your thinking? Are you making judgments before listening? Could you assume positive intent before reacting?

- *Anticipating.* Are you anticipating what to say next while the other person is still talking? Can you instead be fully present and listen attentively?

- *Silence.* How comfortable are you when a conversation drops into silence? Do you feel an urge to jump in and say something, or can you let silence linger?

When you return from a retreat, during which you thought deeply about these questions, select a few people with whom you want to practice deepening conversations. They could be colleagues you want to know better or someone you might tend to cut off. What can you learn from a deeper conversation?

CONTEMPLATION 2:
MAPPING RELATIONSHIPS

This contemplation focuses on the state of your relationships. You are squarely into integral Domain 3—the subjective collective—presented in Chapter 6. Like the spider, you sit at the heart of a web of relationships, some close and others distant, some supportive and others draining.

On a large sheet of paper, draw yourself at the center and your relationships as spokes. Often, the people who are most important in our lives today were introduced by older friends. Mapping these interconnections—who introduced you to whom initially—can be a fascinating exercise. Map:

- The people I live with.
- My close family.

- My inner circle: close friends I call when I am down.
- Current intimate partners.
- Former intimate partners with whom I still have a relationship.
- My second circle: friends that I enjoy spending time with.
- Close colleagues and business associates that I trust.
- My guides: those who support my personal and professional growth.
- My protégés: those that I support and guide in their personal and professional growth.
- My role models and sources of inspiration.
- The departed who have influenced me or who are still present in my dreams.
- My enemies and those who have betrayed me.
- Difficult or toxic colleagues.

Once you have drawn your map, take a moment to reflect. What comes up? Did you imagine you would have so many people or so few people around you? Use pens of different colors to highlight who energizes or inspires you, and who drains you of your energy. Who is supporting you? Whom do you support? Do you want to strengthen your relationship with someone or distance yourself?

CONTEMPLATION 3: EQUANIMITY

Let's take a closer look and observe our relationships through the lenses of impermanence and emptiness.

The notion of friendship is a matter of interpretation. It is a subjective view based on your own inclination toward someone. There is nothing absolute and intrinsic about the goodness or badness of a person—it is only a matter of interpretation. This is what Buddhists call emptiness.

All of our relationships are a matter of perspective. Consider, for example, a young couple who goes on a safari. They walk the path in the bush, hoping to spot some wildlife. To the ants crossing the path as they painstakingly carry food back to the anthill, the woman is a deadly threat who might squash them without even noticing. To the man, the woman is an attractive creature whom he hopes to build a family with when they return home. To the lion hidden in the shadow, the woman is a nice breakfast. It is all a matter of perspective.

Equanimity is maintaining a nonjudgmental and nonreactive attitude. It allows us to see reality with calm and steadiness and to notice our filters of interpretation.

These filters have an evolutionary role. Without them, millions of information bits would bombard our senses and overwhelm us. Look around you. The number of details that you could notice, from the chipped paint on the wall to the color of the tissue box on the table, is infinite. Most details are irrelevant.

We hone an instinctive selectiveness that allows us to concentrate on what matters. We only care about what helps us achieve our goals and obstacles on the way. We interpret the signals we receive and assign labels such as "table" and "tree" to what would otherwise be a senseless wooden structure. We create concepts such as "house" that means "the place where I live." Finally, we attribute characteristics such as good, bad, and neutral to the objects and persons we interact with. We are attracted to friends, we feel aversion toward enemies, and we treat strangers with indifference.

We tend to assume that these characteristics are intrinsic and unchanging. Some people are "bad." They always have been, and will always be. But as we have seen, relationships are subjective and transient. We cycle through the friend/enemy/stranger labels endlessly.

Some of these shifts are archetypal. They have captured our attention since the dawn of humanity. Many movies are based on the enemy-turns-ally story where two adversaries unite to triumph of a common evil. This is also the main plot in many romantic comedies where the leads hate each other at first sight before falling in love.

Friends becoming enemies is another powerful archetype, since God and Satan. We find these narratives in many myths and stories: Cain and Abel, Gandalf and Saruman, or Obi-Wan Kenobi and Anakin Skywalker. It is also the fate of many couples that start as love stories and end in bitter fights.

Everyone who is now a friend or an enemy was once a stranger. Many will return to that status after we lose touch with them.

Equanimity reveals that our perspectives change. These perspectives are also subjective. Every criminal has a parent who loves them. Our nemeses at work have their best friends and lovers. And the strangers we cross in the street have their own web of love and aversion.

Leaders need simple messages to create powerful narratives: this client is good, this competitor is bad, this new employee is good, and the one who just resigned is bad. But there is no permanent or absolute label. This is why the realization of impermanence and emptiness is an important step toward developing equanimity, or nonjudgmental attitude, toward everyone.

To contemplate equanimity, return to the list you created in the first contemplation. Place the names on an attraction-neutral-aversion spectrum. Now remember the stories of these relationships. How did they end up in this category? Are my friends friends to everyone? Who would see them as enemy? Are my enemies enemies for everyone? Who would see them as friend? What new perspectives does this reflection create for you?

CONTEMPLATION 4: COMPASSION

Compassion is not a concept commonly discussed in business schools or the workplace. Even though the people we admire, like Nelson Mandela or the Dalai Lama, lead with compassion, we really want to be Jack Welch or Jeff Bezos. In business, compassion is often viewed in opposition to effectiveness.

Yet compassion is a necessary component of high-performance environments. Compassion, or the wish to reduce the suffering of others, can be found in small, everyday actions and grandiose gestures. It does not lead to accepting underperformance or abandoning tough conversations. On the contrary, a compassionate culture creates transparency. It positively impacts the motivation, engagement, and well-being of employees. It helps reduce stress and anxiety by creating a feeling of psychological safety and trust.

I experienced this culture at McKinsey. The Firm has one of the most ruthless performance evaluation systems with its famous up-or-out policy. Yet it treats those who leave so well that most remain fondly attached to the institution and their former colleagues. Many former McKinsey consultants become McKinsey clients.

Corporate cultures that emphasize individual over collective performance can easily become toxic. They risk destroying the collaboration that is necessary to achieve any business goal. Psychological safety, trust, and compassion are correlated. Hence, leaders play a critical role in shaping a culture that fosters compassion.

Leaders can show compassion in the way they listen and deepen conversations. They take responsibility for the well-being of their colleagues. They attune to the needs of others. They practice nonjudgment and equanimity and do not believe that labels such as friend or enemy are intrinsic and permanent.

It is incredibly hard to show compassion when we are under pressure. Let's say a colleague is underperforming and slowing down the progress of an important project. How can you seek to understand and offer support when your instinct is to get rid of the person? In those moments, you forget your best intentions. You just want to transfer your fear to them.

If the benefits of compassionate leadership are obvious, can we cultivate this quality? Or are some people born with it and others without?

We are all naturally compassionate. Aside from psychopaths, unfortunately well represented in the top echelons, no one likes watching other humans or animals suffer. This built-in mechanism has obvious evolutionary benefits. In the jungle, we are stronger as a tribe than alone.

That said, when you are under pressure, you can easily lose your way and move away from compassion. You can return to it by first having compassion for yourself. You can only see others when you see yourself. You can only connect with others when you show your true self, not a façade.

Leaders are so focused on achieving the mission that they forget to take care of the vehicle that will carry them to their destination. I am always perplexed when I coach leaders who excel at their job yet are so harsh on themselves. They push through the ups and downs of life, relentlessly absorbing shocks, disappointments, setbacks, and grief. How can they give to others when their own sources are depleted?

Let's recognize our pains and deep fears, our crushed hopes and grief, the battles we lost and the mountains we were too scared to climb. Let's hug the lost child and the wounded partner. Let's embrace our suffering and recognize how pathetic and beautiful we all are. You are who you are, in all your beauty, truth, and goodness, with nothing that needs fixing.

Others are just another me. When you see yourself in others, the door of compassion opens. An ancient Tibetan Buddhist practice called Tonglen reduces your ego and increases your natural compassion. Tonglen means "give and take." The practice consists of using the breath as a vehicle to visualize compassion in action. On the in-breath, you take in the suffering of others. On the out-breath, you send them relief, peace, joy, and well-being. You can direct the practice at one person or a community. It is like a prayer but instead of praying for an outer force to reduce suffering, you take matters into your own hands.

Tonglen helps us fight the tendency to seek pleasure and avoid pain. Even though the practice is symbolic, you may note a resistance or a contraction at the idea of taking in the suffering of someone else. Let's just observe it and sit with it for a moment. Over time, this inquiry helps to develop fearlessness. By opening your heart, you no longer feel the need to tense and protect yourself.

You can follow this guide to practice Tonglen and grow in compassion:

Sit comfortably and take a few centering breaths. Bring yourself into a state of equanimity, peace, and clarity.

Bring to mind the person or the community who you want to extend compassion to. Appreciate the suffering they are experiencing.

Imagine their suffering, pain, and challenges as a thick, black, heavy, warm smoke. Picture your own well-being, comfort, strength, and stability as a light, white-blue, cool air.

Now, start exchanging through the breath.

On the in-breath, visualize absorbing the dark, dense smoke, representing suffering, distress, anxiety, and sadness. On the outbreath, visualize sending pure clear air, representing love, peace, and relief.

Find your rhythm. Alternate between absorbing the dark clouds of suffering and sending back a pure, cool, white cloud of well-being.

SUMMARY

Great relationships are initially built through conversation. To deepen your relationships, you must give your full attention to the other person. This allows you to build intimacy, explore possibilities, and plan action.

You must be aware of the three main destructors of relationships: interruptions, hyper-efficiency, and polarization. To fight these, these contemplations help with deepening conversations, mapping your relationships, and developing equanimity and compassion.

ADDITIONAL JOURNALING
AND REFLECTIONS

- With whom did I connect today? What made that connection possible?
- Who do I listen to? Who listens to me?
- What do I bring to my relationships?
- For what do I depend on others? For what do others depend on me? How do I ask for help?
- Who is a friend I am missing?
- Who loves me?
- Who knows me?
- Whom am I grateful for?
- Whom do I want to apologize to? Why can't I?
- What becomes possible when I trust? Where do I find the courage to trust?
- What becomes possible when I don't interrupt? When I am not interrupted (by others, by my devices)?
- Whom do I not need in my life anymore?

Chapter 9

DANCING *with* COMPLEXITY

I N THE PREVIOUS TWO CHAPTERS, WE EXPLORED CON-
templations to connect with ourselves and others. Making
sense of the world is our next inquiry.

From the moment we are born, we try to make sense of the
world around us. We observe through our five senses. We interpret and compare. Finally, we create stories that explain why
good and bad things happen around us. We form our worldview
through trial and error. We settle on interpretations that serve
us well. Collectively, what we call culture is really an interpretation of how to be in the world. The more we share in making meaning, the more seamlessly we can operate together as a
group or society.

THE SHAMAN AND THE CEO

Leaders, too, are responsible for creating meaning. They have more experience and access to information. They are in a better position to create a narrative that explains why the company lost a contract or gained market share or why merging with a competitor is a great move.

Great leaders organize our world. Justin Menkes, an expert in leadership assessment, writes in a *Harvard Business Review* article titled "Three Traits Every CEO Needs," "Leaders who can find order in chaos find taking on multidimensional problems invigorating and are distinguished by their ability to bring clarity to quandaries that baffle others."

The village shaman explains why now is a good time to hunt for a mammoth. The CEO convinces her board to launch a digital transformation. Both create narratives to explain the order of the world. The shaman lives in a simple universe paced by the seasons. His KPIs are about food, safety, health, and cohesion of the tribe. The CEO lives in a complex universe made of abundant data and infinite permutations. Unfortunately for the CEO, she has a similar brain structure to that of the tribe shaman who lived 30,000 years ago.

Creating meaning goes beyond elaborating forecasts or devising great strategies. It is about understanding the fundamental nature of the phenomena we are witnessing. This allows us to lead our teams accordingly. Wrong interpretations can have catastrophic consequences for the organizations we lead, just like sending a hunting party into enemy territory would be disastrous for the tribe.

Despite vast amounts of data and computing power, our primitive brains often make the wrong decisions because we fail to grasp the complexity of the world around us. We're constantly catching up. We tend to oversimplify, and we fall prey to many cognitive biases.

For example, technological change is often misinterpreted as a gradual evolution when it in fact transforms industries rapidly. Many companies failed to see this and paid heavy consequences. Kodak missed digital photography, Nokia missed smartphones, and Toys R Us and Borders missed e-commerce.

Change happens in all industries. We saw in the previous chapter that impermanence is a constant. Traditional airlines reacted too late to the rise of budget travel. U.S. car manufacturers missed the rise of Japanese and Korean competitors. Entire business models collapsed when new competitors brought more convenience to customers.

The outside world is not the only challenge we face. Organizations create their own complexity. We have built systems that we do not understand anymore. How many corporate transformations fail despite the brilliant shaman brains that designed them? Most mergers do not deliver their expected benefits. The spreadsheets and PowerPoint presentations fail to capture the complexity of the humans who make the businesses run. Failed mergers, such as Chrysler and Daimler, AOL and Time Warner, or Air France and KLM, show that financial projections miss the full picture. Leaders take comfort in the simplicity of these projections, but they miss the complexity of human nature.

How can we explain the discrepancy between our extraordinary body of knowledge and our failure to grasp natural phenomena? Science allows us to put satellites in orbit, build 100-story towers, and transplant hearts. Yet we fail to control a virus, and the world plunges into chaos.

REDUCTIONISM

Modern management offers a reductionist view of the world. We simplify problems and reduce them into manageable parts. We make assumptions about the market and the competition. We generate forecasts, budgets, and performance indicators. At that point, we feel strong because we believe that we are in control of the future. Our beautiful Excel sheets and PowerPoints give us certainty that we know the future.

Reductionism stems from the development of science during the Renaissance. It accelerated with the industrial revolution, Frederick Taylor's "scientific management" principles, modern accounting, business schools, management consultants, and the quest for shareholder value. Reductionism expresses our immense desire for certainty and our ever-increasing aversion to risk.

In our quest for predictability, we want to dominate what was once out of our control: the seasons, the cycles of day and night, the weather, and our fellow living beings. And to obtain security, food, and resources, we have eliminated most wild animals. The living vertebrate animals on the planet today are mainly destined for food consumption. We slaughter 70 billion land animals every year.[1] We have depleted 90 percent of large fish stocks.[2] A third of forests are gone to make space for intensive farming.[3] We even coined the term "Nature Deficit Disorder" after a study sponsored by the Bureau of Land Management discovered that American kids recognize over a thousand corporate logos but can hardly name local plants or animals.

Unfortunately, reductionism ignores the long-term impact of our actions. If we could consider systems in their entirety, across space and time, we would realize that what we call predictable on a small-term scale has wildly unpredictable effects. How will we inhabit a world without oceans, forests, glaciers, and wildlife?

COMPLICATED VS. COMPLEX

To make sense of the world, we need the right vocabulary. David Snowden, a former researcher at IBM, introduced a crucial distinction in the late nineties: complicated vs. complex.

---

1 https://faunalytics.org/global-animal-slaughter-statistics-and-charts/
2 https://unctad.org/news/90-fish-stocks-are-used-fisheries-subsidies-must-stop
3 https://ourworldindata.org/deforestation#the-world-has-lost-one-third-of-its-forests-but-an-end-of-deforestation-is-possible

We can predict complicated systems as long as we know their current state and the rules that govern the behaviors of their parts. For example, a photocopy machine is complicated. It integrates decades of research and expertise across several disciplines such as mechanical engineering, optics, laser and ink technologies, and computer science. But when I press the green button, it produces the same result all the time. I get a copy of the document I put on the glass. I may not understand why or how, but the experts do.

Since the invention of the wheelbarrow and printing press, we have mastered complicated technologies. We produce reliable results, like our photocopy machine. Assembly lines, oil drilling and refining, powerplants and electricity transmission, steelmaking, personal computers, mobile phones, internet, airplanes, photography, modern medicine, vaccination, the pill, high-speed trains, skyscrapers, water treatment and sanitation—they're all complicated but predictable.

We love complicated problems because they satisfy our craving for predictability. Unfortunately, not all problems are complicated; some are complex. Complex problems do not lend themselves to a reductionist approach. Throwing more expertise at them doesn't help.

In his book *At Home in the Universe*, American professor Stuart Kauffman writes, "The reductionist program has been spectacularly successful, and will continue to be so. But it has often left a vacuum....The deep difficulty here lies in the fact that the complex whole may exhibit properties that are not readily explained by understanding the parts."

We face complex phenomena when we are unable to connect causes and effects. Capital markets, pandemics, elections, organization cultures, and consumer demand are complex. The dynamics of complex systems entail large numbers of elements interacting in nonlinear ways. Acting on one part of the system can trigger unexpected consequences in other parts.

If you run a chain of yoga studios, you know that dropping your membership fee by 10 percent is likely to result in an increase of new clients, and adding a new dynamic class at lunch time is likely to attract the young, sport-minded office crowd. You may not know exactly the sales that will result from one action versus the other, but you have a sense of the general effects. At the other end of the spectrum, when you launch a totally new product (for example, dog yoga, where clients can bring their canine companions to a yoga practice), you have no idea whether you will attract a hundred clients or zero.

There are many cases where poorly understood causality leads to disastrous consequences. In public policy, for example, penalizing the consumption of recreational drugs sends drug sales to the black market, enabling a subterranean economy to flourish and boosting the sales of more dangerous and powerful drugs. Complex systems have many interrelated factors that make cause and effect unpredictable.

When United Airlines forcefully removed a paying passenger from a plane to allow airline employees to board, they thought they were dealing with a complicated problem of operational effectiveness. The event backfired and triggered massive reputational damage on social media. This is complexity at work.

Snowden and his co-writer consultant Mary Boone summarize it in their seminal *Harvard Business Review* article titled "A Leader's Framework for Decision Making."

In a complicated context, at least one right answer exists. In a complex context, however, right answers can't be ferreted out. It's like the difference between, say, a Ferrari and the Brazilian rainforest. Ferraris are complicated machines, but an expert mechanic can take one apart and reassemble it without changing a thing. The car is static, and the whole is the sum of its parts. The rainforest, on the other hand, is in constant flux—a species becomes extinct, weather patterns change, an agricultural project reroutes a water source—and the whole is far more than the sum of its parts. This is the realm of "unknown unknowns," and it is the domain to which much of contemporary business has shifted.

It is only by raising our level of consciousness and discernment that we can recognize complexity and finally make sense of the world. When you are too busy to pause and reflect, you see every problem as complicated and continue living in delusion.

GREATER DISCERNMENT

Janet Drey is the Managing Director at the Consortium for Contemplative Leadership. She told me about her personal experience with retreats and how leaders can build greater discernment.

My own retreat experience started when I was a young adult. I grew up Catholic, but my mother's faith included meditation. She was ahead of her time. She gave me permission early on to explore my inner life. A lot of religions are about beliefs but we're not talking about beliefs here, we're talking about a relationship with ourselves, with the divine, with nature, and with others. It doesn't matter where we start with those four, as one often leads to the other three. Even when people don't name the sacred, in spiritual or religious terms, they will eventually find some way for the transcendent to come into their search.

For me, the retreat experience began small, an hour or two in nature, with prayer time. Later, in my thirties, as I had to balance work with raising a family, I started scheduling regular time away. I used to call them "desert days."

There was a woman in my city who organized these regular retreat days. She would start with a theme that we would explore together as a group for maybe forty-five minutes. Then she would send us off to spend the day on our own. The day, for me, was about unpacking what I had accumulated. I would slow my mind down, turn into my body, and sometimes I would just feel the tiredness that was there. I would simply rest and take a nap. That was part of the retreat and it was wonderful. I would also explore recent emotional experiences and I would take time to journal, to go deeper than maybe what my initial response to a situation would be.

I continued this practice of taking a day a month. Sometimes, I could not give it a whole day, perhaps only half a day. Sometimes, I would retreat over a weekend. In order not to disrupt my family, I would leave in the morning and be home the same night. That regular retreat time became very precious.

I realized how much these retreats were as much part of my work as my regular day-to-day. I did not consider it personal time, it was really work time that I would take out of the office, and I would always come back more productive. I felt more clearheaded and grounded, month after month. I was really looking forward to this time away.

Those retreats were about learning tools like discernment. This was not only of benefit for me in my personal life, but it would also improve my decision-making as a leader. Facing complex situations, I would step out, pull back, and give attention to what I might not have initially considered. I would observe how things were related to one another and where my attachments were keeping me from making good decisions.

Discernment can apply to an external issue or it can be much more subtle and personal. We can explore where we might be attached to outcomes or maintaining a façade that is important to one's identity.

A big area leaders can explore is ego. There are areas that they naturally feel successful about and areas, like attachments, that are in the shadow. These may not even be in their field of awareness at first. Pausing to discern, becoming aware of these shadows, can influence their decision-making. But to do that, leaders must create a safe space and go slowly. On a retreat, we come willing to open the door a little and peek into how we might be contributing to recurring issues or how we respond in ways that are not working as well as they used to.

By going on retreats, leaders may notice patterns, for example, how they work with others, areas they avoid, areas that cause conflicts. This deepening awareness is an invitation for personal growth. We can observe how we have structured our lives after maybe a couple of decades of successful work. With greater awareness, we may be more willing to go off track, to try new ways of being and being present, instead of staying where we have found success to date. We can give more attention to the underdeveloped aspects of our personality. This may make us feel vulnerable but contributes greatly to our wholeness.

This may not be beginner's material; we need to be willing to look deeper. The initial value of a retreat is just to open that door. Instead of going, going, going, we learn to be still and listen to what is going on within us; we slow the mind and the body down. Once we do that, new things rise to the surface.

Janet's experience reflects what I heard from many leaders who go on regular retreats. When we dwell in silence and still-ness, it becomes easier to grasp the whole system and challenge simplistic reductionism. We no longer need to yield to the tyranny of making predictions. We can let go and start again with a fresh mind.

Four contemplations will help you dance with complexity. The first contemplation is about recognizing complexity and not mistaking it for complicatedness. The second is about noticing the phenomenon of emergence around us. The third is about Not-Knowing. The last is about immersing ourselves in nature and becoming one with complexity.

CONTEMPLATION 1:
RECOGNIZING COMPLEXITY

In this contemplation, you will practice differentiating compli-catedness from complexity.

Many questions can be solved with the right amount of data, expertise, and experience. We break problems down in simple elements and analyze each part independently. We follow clear steps and obtain predictable results. Imagine flying a modern commercial airliner. This is extraordinarily complicated. Aviation technology benefits from 120 years of development since the first flight by the Wright brothers. Yet, the process is also predictable and replicable by thousands of pilots around the world each day.

Not all problems can be broken down in such a way. Let's imagine now the merger of two companies with complementary products and footprints. The two CEOs have convinced their boards. The synergies have been quantified by the management consultants. The investment bankers have created a mechanism for the exchange of shares. There's even a nice investor presentation explaining how this bright future will be achieved thanks to impeccable planning.

In their eager reductionist thinking, the architects of the merger are solving what they perceive as a complicated problem. They ignore the complexity of the situation.

How will the two cultures interact? Will key executives embrace the plan? What political alliances will be created? How will competitors and clients react? How will employees change their behaviors in the face of layoffs? How will this affect the competitiveness of the merged entity? Is the connection between the systems, organizations, and processes as easy as depicted by the consultants? Will management get a clear picture of what is really happening?

In general, physical, inert systems are complicated, and living organisms, such as organizations, societies, and ecosystems, are complex. Designing a mobile phone is complicated; raising a child is complex. Launching a rocket to the moon is complicated; fighting a pandemic is complex.

Leaders often fail to recognize complexity. After all, they are paid to have certainties not doubts. And when they have doubts, they may share them with their spouses, coaches, or therapists, but not with their boards and even less with their subordinates. Pride outweighs humility.

Four criteria signal that we face complexity and not complicatedness: lack of clear causality, nonlinearity, a whole greater than the sum of its parts, and lack of repeatability.

Take an issue that you are facing and set a period of reflection of at least a couple of hours. Reflect and journal on the following questions:

- Do I understand the relationship between causes and effects? Do I know for sure what factors cause what effects?

You may not always know the exact proportions in which one factor influences another, but do you even have a sense of the direction your critical outputs will move when you act on your main inputs?

- Are the relationships between inputs and outputs linear?

If you increase the size of your sales force or decrease your pricing, will you boost sales in a proportionate amount? Do small variations in your inputs create similarly small variations in the outputs?

Sometimes, we face nonlinearity. Adoption of new technology is often exponential. A small decrease in hourly wage can result in a prolonged strike instead of a decline of personnel cost. Complex systems often exhibit discontinuities or disruptions when small input variations cause unpredictable effects.

- Can the system be broken down into independent parts?

An automobile is a sophisticated piece of equipment, but its systems, while connected, operate largely independently from one another. I can change a wheel without touching the engine, and a failure of the windshield wipers won't affect the fuel line. On the other hand, a forest is a complex system in equilibrium. Killing one species can lead to another species proliferating and becoming a nuisance. The various components of the forest do not operate independently from one another, and the multiple links that connect them are not obvious even after a careful analysis.

- Can an action be repeated with the same results each time?

Typically, complicated systems exhibit repeatability traits and the same actions produce similar effects. The word processor on which I am typing this book has benefited from drastic improvements since its first version in 1983. Yet, it is a highly predictable system and the same key sequence always produces the same effects. In contrast, complex systems do not. Two siblings, even twins, raised in the same way by the same parents, may exhibit radically different characters, interests, careers, and sexual orientation.

CONTEMPLATION 2: EMERGENCE

The epistemological impossibility to know with certainty the relationships between cause and effect is a marker of complex systems. In other words, no advances in science, data processing, philosophy, or spirituality can ever allow us to anticipate how a system will behave.

Complex systems evolve in their own unpredictable way. This is not chaos, though; patterns do emerge. The wind draws waves and shapes dunes in the desert. A forest organizes itself around vegetal and animal species. A civilization develops and cultures come to life.

We can observe and explain the results with hindsight but never with foresight. This is why experts excel at explaining the past but not at predicting the future. It doesn't matter whether it is in the field of sports, weather patterns, economics, capital markets, global terrorism, or politics. Those who can predict the future of complex systems are few and probably lucky.

The emergence of patterns in complex systems often leaves us in awe. Believers see the hand of God in nature, human consciousness, the shapes of clouds, or the variety in the animal realm. Indeed, what is spirituality, if not the recognition that the forces that shape our world and human experience are beyond what our reductionist thinking can fathom?

Emergence is a characteristic of living systems. Life, consciousness, evolution of species, societies, cities, political systems, languages, and cultures all emerge, create patterns, and organize themselves through trillions of random interactions every day. Out of seeming randomness, order emerges. Yet, no amount of data, science, knowledge, or expertise can predict what this order will look like ahead of time.

Sometimes, we believe we can score a victory over emergence by influencing it. Mankind has always sought to dominate nature, in a bid to secure food, safety, and shelter for its growing populations. At one point in the twentieth century, we may even have thought that we won. We only ignored the unanticipated, long-term consequences of our actions.

Examples of unintended consequences abound. Prohibition of alcohol and recreational drugs leads to higher consumption and the emergence of organized crime. Efforts by educators and churches to promote abstinence among teens leads to higher pregnancy rates. Increasing the severity and frequency of prison sentences increases criminality. The introduction of new animals, such as rabbits in Australia or starlings in Central Park, can lead to severe disturbances to ecosystems.

We must accept that we are not gods but Mickey Mouse in

The Sorcerer's Apprentice, unleashing chain reactions that we do not understand.

In this contemplation, reflect on all the occurrences of emergence that you can witness in your surroundings or in your immediate professional experience.

You may start by taking a walk in nature and observing the emergence of motifs everywhere: the leaves on a tree, the petals of flowers, the organization of an anthill, honeycombs, or the waves at the surface of a mountain stream.

Notice how your perspective on emergence changes with the scale of your observation. From the infinitely small to the universe at large, design patterns are specific to that level of examination. Galaxies emerge, stars emerge, and on the surface of our planet, cloud systems emerge.

Journal about your experience of emergence.

CONTEMPLATION 3:
NOT-KNOWING

Zen masters emphasize Not-Knowing to clear our minds from garbage. This keeps us open to fresh perspectives. Not-Knowing is at odds with our reductionist culture and the mindset of most leaders. Leaders must know. They are paid to know. Recognizing that they don't know is not a career-enhancing move. But pretending to know when we don't runs against the important quality of authenticity.

We must find a balance. We practice Not-Knowing as a posture of humility. It is the only possible answer to complexity. We can force complicated problems into submission with intellect, data, and experience. But these tools are useless in the face of complexity. Humility and Not-Knowing are more powerful.

Humility doesn't mean inaction or paralysis. Humility is mustering the courage to admit that we don't know. When faced with complexity, conventional leaders react with denial. They mobilize more resources to crack the problem. Contemplative leaders accept complexity with humility. They embrace their inability to predict and adopt an explorer mindset. They design small, probing experiments to start figuring out how the system responds.

Christian mystic Meister Eckhart wrote: "Be willing to be a beginner every single morning." Beginners are comfortable with Not-Knowing and the impossibility of knowing. It is this admission that allows you to relax and think clearly and creatively. You can probe, experiment, and pilot. Small-scale pilots and experiments tell you how the system responds. You can, through trial and error, design new experiments. You make mistakes and learn from them. You fall and get back on your feet, as many times as necessary. Progressively, you learn more about the whole phenomenon. The small failures of yesterday are your best protection against the major crashes of tomorrow.

Ultimately, as you embrace complexity, you build trust in your capacity for acceptance. It is the fundamental step to fully accept reality without resistance. This is a gesture of power, not weakness, and should not be confused with resignation and fatalism.

In this contemplation, choose a complex problem you must confront and reflect on the following questions:

- Am I willing to admit that I don't know? Am I willing to consider that I cannot know, that no amount of additional data, expertise, or resources will lead me to the right answer? How does that feel? What fears arise? In what other circumstances have I been confronted with situations that were more complex than my ability to know?
- When I admit that I don't know and cannot know, do I get a sense of release and liberation?

If you still sense that you should know, perhaps you are right and the issue you are contemplating is complicated, not complex. In that case, it lends itself to problem-solving.

- Ask a new set of questions:
    ◦ When I look at the data, what is it that I expect not to find? What surprises me?
    ◦ What am I explaining away? What am I avoiding?
    ◦ What would happen if I shifted one core assumption?
    ◦ Whose perspectives am I not considering? What voices am I not listening to? Who else could I

invite to look at this problem with me? A supplier, a customer, a front-line employee? A poet, a philosopher, a psychologist? A spiritual guide?

People coming from diverse horizons will bring radically new perspectives that may shed light on a complex system. Even though we all love living in an echo chamber, can you also invite people who usually have opposite views from yours?

- What if I looked at the entire system, instead of just the aspects that concern me?

Looking at the parts is not sufficient because the system is greater than just the sum of its parts.

- What experiments and probes can I devise to test the system and see how it responds?

CONTEMPLATION 4:
MEDITATION IN NATURE

As kids, we all spent time lying on our backs, gazing at the sky. Perhaps we played on the beach or in the woods during our summer vacations. Sometimes, we lose our connection to nature as we grow older. Yet, nature is our source, and for millions of years, we developed in close connection with it. The elements determined our hunting, gathering, and migration strategies. The scent in the air might have indicated food, rain, or danger.

You may convince yourself that you do not need to connect with nature anymore. Our physical and virtual shopping malls are open 24/7 and our homes, offices, and cities always bright. You can become oblivious of the sun, moon, and seasons.

For this contemplation, choose a comfortable place in nature, where you can sit in awe, just like you did when you were a child. And with the innocence of the child, use all your senses: listen, observe, smell, touch, and taste.

This is where you come from. This is where you belong. Nature is the Great Mother, the source of our nurturing. Let go of your thoughts, plans, control, and narratives for a moment. No more doing, only being. Nature helps us understand complexity, recognize emergence, and accept that we don't and can't know everything.

Watch the stars and feel the immensity of the universe and how little we know.

Watch the clouds and realize impermanence. Nothing remains; everything changes.

Watch the rainstorm, lying down on the ground, letting the drops fall on your face, and inviting the elements to cleanse you.

The wind takes away your worries, stress, and anger.

Watch the mountains and realize how insignificant we are.

The forest is the source of life, which nurtures and protects.

The rhythm and sound of the waves crashing on the coast bring you into a quiet trance.

Nature is always here, always our teacher.

Now go and dance with complexity.

SUMMARY

To lead effectively, leaders must make sense of the world. Often, we are conditioned to see every phenomenon as complicated, suitable to be modelized with our standard deterministic approach. The reality is that many phenomena are complex and do not lend themselves to a deterministic description. Only by building greater discernment can we recognize complexity.

Complex systems have no immediate relationships between cause and effect; they are nonlinear, nonrepeatable, and the whole is greater than its parts. Consequently, they produce or behave by patterns, called emergence, that are not determinable in advance.

To dance with complexity, we must cultivate the Not-Knowing mind and approach the phenomenon through small experiments and probes. The only possible response in the face of complexity is humility.

ADDITIONAL JOURNALING
AND REFLECTIONS

- What do I know for sure?
- What did I use to know for sure that turned out to be wrong?

- What surprised me today? How did I respond?
- How do I resist in the face of uncertainty or the unknown and the unknowable?
- What do I not know that I would love to know? Can I find out? Can I live with not knowing? What will getting more information change?
- Have I seen this pattern before?
- Can I differentiate between resignation and acceptance in the face of what I don't control?
- Can I see the whole system? Can I see the forest for the trees?
- What will be the impact of my actions in one year, five years, ten years?

DANCING WITH COMPLEXITY

Chapter 10

EMBRACING
DEATH

I N THE PREVIOUS THREE CHAPTERS, WE BUILT THE
foundation of contemplative leadership. We've developed
the capacity for inner and outer connections, and making sense
of the world. The remaining three chapters address key messages
of spiritual traditions. These are intimately connected to human
development. In this chapter, we will discuss and contemplate
death, our ultimate teacher. We will explore the other two, wisdom and purpose, in the next chapters.

Most people don't want to think or talk about death. There
is nothing fun about dying. Ribur Rinpoche, a Tibetan master,
approached the topic head on. He taught on death and rebirth
and pointed out that people in the West don't want to hear about

their own ending. "This is wrong," he claimed. "This is very wrong. At the time of death, we don't want to be sad...It is now, while we are alive, that we have to think about it. In this way, we have to think about it correctly, and to make the right preparation..."

We behave as if we were going to live forever. We squander our time with mindless activities, watching reality TV or cat videos, wasting endless hours on social media. We work in unsatisfying jobs and attend dinner parties that bore us. Few adults continue developing themselves once they set out in life. No more learning, no more reading, no more reflecting. Most freak out at the thought of spending one quiet hour alone and immediately seek a distraction. It is as if they were trying to avoid the reality of the present moment by keeping busy.

We only have a finite number of hours to live. We don't know how many. This is a reality no one likes to contemplate. It is easy to watch war movies but difficult to reflect on our own mortality. In past centuries, death was an everyday companion. In 1800, between a third and half of children did not reach the age of five. Life expectancy in Europe was less than forty years. Today, Western societies hide their old, sick, and dead. We avoid reminding anyone that death is the eternal companion of life.

Frank Ostaseski, cofounder of the Zen Hospice Project, writes in *The Five Invitations*, "Death is not waiting for us at the end of a long road. Death is always with us, in the marrow of every passing moment. She is the secret teacher hiding in plain sight, helping us to discover what matters most."

Instead of walking hand in hand with death, we look the other way and pretend we will live forever. Terrified by reality, we resort to three strategies. First, we numb ourselves with endless work and distractions. Second, we invent a fantasy world in which appearance, wealth, and status are all that matter. Finally, we pursue immortality projects that outlast us. We produce children, we build companies or castles, or we write poetry or compose music. Some donate money in exchange for their name on the wall of a library or concert hall.

Poet and spiritual teacher Stephen Levine writes in *A Year to Live*: "We are motivated more by aversion to the unpleasant than by a will toward truth, freedom, or healing. We are constantly attempting to escape our life, to avoid rather than enter our pain, and we wonder why it is so difficult to be fully alive."

I noticed that those who have a close encounter with death tend to have a renewed appetite for life. Whether they survive a near-death experience, an illness, or an airplane crash, they are content and grateful for the daily joys that others ignore. Nothing like staring death in the eyes to realize what matters. But there is no need to have a brush with death. You can make it the focus of our contemplation now.

I sometimes bring up the topic of death in my retreats. Once we pierce through the initial discomfort that the subject triggers, I notice that participants relax. You can resist the idea of your own death, like you resist complexity (see Chapter 9). To progress on this journey, you need to follow your usual contemplative inquiry. First, acknowledge reality, explore your discomfort, and then embrace it. Acceptance always supersedes fear.

Contemplating death is an integral part of all spiritual traditions. Sometimes, a dogma lurks in the shadows. The possibility of an afterlife can be a carrot and stick to steer us toward a virtuous character. Whether it is the promise of eternal bliss, a good rebirth, or the threat of hell, we live a moral life today to reap our rewards tomorrow. But dogma is not necessary to the contemplation of death and a moral existence. We can realize that doing what is right and meaningful carries its own rewards in the present moment.

In the introduction of his book *The Road to Character*, American columnist David Brooks distinguishes résumé virtues and eulogy virtues: "The résumé virtues are the ones you list on your résumé, the skills that you bring to the job market and that contribute to external success. The eulogy virtues are deeper. They're the virtues that get talked about at your funeral, the ones that exist at the core of your being—whether you are kind, brave, honest or faithful; what kind of relationships you formed."

Even though our culture emphasizes résumé virtues, we know that eulogy virtues matter, too. They bring us fulfillment and a sense of accomplishment and completion while we are alive.

This distinction between résumé and eulogy virtues is critical to cultivate contemplative leadership. The two are not opposing forces: they complement each other like yin and yang. Leaders need to make sure that their organizations get to live another day, and also have a positive, long-term impact on the world.

As a leader, you will benefit greatly from contemplating death. The following contemplations will place the short-term challenges of daily life in a long-term perspective. They will bring what truly matters to the forefront. And they will help you clarify the values and purpose that should underpin the work of your life—your opus magnum. In the end, contemplating death focuses your mind on the life you want to live.

CONTEMPLATION 1:
OBSERVING DEATH AROUND US

Remembering death is a powerful antidote to taking yourself too seriously. Keep in mind that your presence on Earth is only temporary. There will be a time when you are no longer here. This is not advocating that you should be reckless, fatalistic, or indifferent, as nihilists would suggest. It is not that nothing matters. Instead, many things matter, and you should place your attention on those things that matter most.

Let's say you have an axe to grind with a colleague on the executive committee who is not supporting your proposal. This is an opportunity to recognize that this, too, shall pass. There are more important ways to spend the rest of your day than brooding about it. You might start by calling someone you love to tell them you love them. That simple little act of turning to love rather than hate may help you find constructive ways to deal with your colleague.

There's a joke that very few executives on their death bed wish they had spent more time in the office. We see the humor in that saying but often fail to apply its lessons. How many late hours and business trips prevent you from seeing your kids grow? How many weekend conference calls have deprived you of opportunities to engage with your loved ones? How many wasted hours leave you too drained to pursue meaningful activities?

We always believe that there will be another opportunity. But one day, you realize that the last chance you had to call a parent has passed. Your kids have grown. Your physical performance has declined. It hits you that you will never have the career of your dreams. You have settled for expediency.

In the Hindu epic *Mahabharata*, Yaksha, a quirky nature trickster spirit, quizzes the hero Yudhisthira: "What is the greatest wonder in this world?" Yudhisthira answers: "Day after day countless people die. Yet those who remain believe they will live forever. What can be a greater wonder?"

In this first contemplation, go for a quiet walk and observe death all around you. Buddhist monks meditate in cemeteries or charnel grounds. There is no need to go that far. You can see death in nature, as leaves fall from the trees, flowers decay, and insects and worms are eaten by birds. It is in the graveyards around our churches and temples. It is in the news. Open a paper and read the obituaries. Death is everywhere in our food stores, where the flesh of dead animals is packaged for our consumption.

Observe the ubiquity of death. Journal about your experience when you return to your retreat place.

CONTEMPLATION 2: HOW MANY DAYS LEFT?

Even though its meaning is clear, I have never been a fan of Gandhi's quote, "Live as if you were to die tomorrow." The essence of being a leader is precisely to act as if we were going to live beyond tomorrow. Planning and delaying gratification ensures that we behave responsibly and create a better tomorrow. The ability to imagine and conceptualize the future is a human characteristic. But how much longer do we have exactly?

Let's do some quick math. Imagine you will live until the age of eighty or eighty-five. That is a reasonable assumption for healthy, middle-aged adults in the developed world. Multiply the years you have left by 365 to get the days you have left.

Therefore, a forty-year-old might be left with 14,600 days to live. This sounds like a lot, but it really is not. This will go fast if you numb yourself working without purpose, spending time away from those you love, or wasting hours on social media.

How do you use these days? Time is like money; you can choose to invest it or spend it. What do you do with your time? Do you invest in yourself or in others, focusing on professional and personal growth? Or do you engage in consumption, generating momentary pleasures? Or do you simply try to "kill time" because you have too much of it?

In this second contemplation, estimate the days you may have left and break down this time between these major buckets. You can also create or add your own categories.

- Time for growth: learning, exploring, creating, reading, studying, spiritual quest.
- Time for love: spending meaningful time with loved ones and close friends, caring for others, raising kids.
- Time for health: sleeping, eating, exercising, regular checkups.
- Time for the community: building businesses, leading others, supporting causes, filing your tax returns.
- Time spent oiling the mechanics of life: commuting, working, shopping for or cleaning the house, fixing things, paying bills.
- Time spent relaxing and unwinding.
- Time wasted.

These definitions are very personal. What is wasted time for one is meaningful to someone else. Some activities may belong to several categories. For example, take a game of golf. Is it an investment in health, an effort to build relationships, an excuse to get away from home? Should your work be considered a necessary chore because you need the money, or is it your contribution to society? This is the beauty of this contemplation: you get to choose the meaning you ascribe to the hours you live.

When you are done, journal with your reflections. What implicit or explicit tradeoffs do you make? How much of your time is under your control? How enjoyable or meaningful is every hour? What could you change to better balance time allocation?

CONTEMPLATION 3:
THE NINE-POINT MEDITATION ON DEATH

This contemplation is inspired by the Lamrim, the traditional Tibetan step-by-step path to the ultimate realization of liberation. It is a didactic arrangement of the teachings of the Buddha and a roadmap that guides practitioners toward enlightenment.

The contemplation of death plays an important role in the Lamrim. I have adapted this traditional meditation to the context of leadership. There are three sections. First, we reflect on the inevitability of death. Second, on the uncertainty of the time of death. Third, on the fact that only a contemplative approach can help at the time of death.

Block a couple of hours for this meditation and have your journal ready. This contemplation is a difficult one. We are so used to avoiding death that dedicating time to explore its implications may result in feeling uncomfortable. It is also a contemplation that will push you to a greater stage of consciousness.

Releasing our attachments is the primary key to unlock our freedom to act and lead with purpose.

Take a few moments to settle in a comfortable chair. Let the mind quiet in the present moment and bring your awareness to the breath. Set an intention for this contemplation. For example: "May this meditation allow my leadership to bring positive impact to myself, those close to me, and my broader community."

Now, contemplate each of the following three sections.

Part 1: The Inevitability of Death

- *Point 1:* I accept that everyone will die. Death is the natural consequence of birth, and no one will escape it. Great leaders have had fabulous destinies, wielded enormous power, achieved immense fortunes, and been wildly respected. Yet even they have died. I think of all the famous leaders I admire. They brought tremendous energy to their endeavors, impacted the lives of many, and overcame setbacks and adversity. Eventually, they all died. No one is immortal.

- *Point 2:* The end of my life nears continuously. Every second that passes brings me closer to my death. Time never stops. It is only up to me how I use the capital I have left. Slowly, second after second, day after day, month after month, year after year, the clock is ticking until it reaches zero. Some day will be the last of my life.

- *Point 3:* The time I must dedicate to my opus magnum—
  my purpose on Earth—is limited. Accomplishing my
  goal with dignity, morality, and authenticity will produce
  positive ripples long after I am gone. How I act today
  impacts the world of tomorrow. Will I do what is
  right? The best way to be an impactful leader and give
  meaning to my life is to become aware of how I spend my
  time. As I return to the buckets of time in the previous
  contemplation, I ask: how do I want to rearrange my
  priorities?

In conclusion, the time to start shaping and embodying your
values and purpose to have a positive impact around you is now.
Don't wait.

Part II: The Uncertainty of the Time of Death

Perhaps you know intellectually that you are going to die, but
you believe that death is a long way away. You have plenty of time.

- *Point 4:* I acknowledge life is uncertain. There is no rhyme
  or reason to the time of our death or how we die. We
  have statistics and life expectancy tables. But I am not
  an average person nor a statistic. I look around and see
  plenty of randomness and unpredictability. The rich and
  powerful may die before modest people. The healthy may
  die before the sick. The young may die before the old.

Death can catch me at any time. I can plan to live a long life if I take care of myself, but there is never any certainty.

- *Point 5:* There are many ways to die. About half of the deaths in the U.S. are caused by heart disease, cancer, and accidents. Despite our risk-averse society and the great progress of medicine, there are still so many more ways to die. We talk about stupid ways to die. Is there ever an intelligent death? I'll take a moment to reflect on all the people I know who died recently and contemplate the many ways to die.

- *Point 6:* Our life is very fragile. From the moment I was born, my body has been decaying. As I age, I feel my energy going down. My endurance, strength, and mobility diminish. (Personally, I could go partying all night long in my twenties, and now I need two days to recover from a hangover. I could fly across time zones without noticing, and now I need a week to adjust my body clock again.) This body is fragile and will not last forever. I can slow the tide with proper nutrition, exercise, sleep, relationships, and engagement in my work, but I cannot turn back the clock.

By reflecting on these three points, you recognize that now is the time to start working on your opus magnum.

Part III: A Contemplative Practice of Leadership
Is the Best Way to Sustain My Effort and Leave a Legacy

You want to leave a vibrant legacy by thinking and acting right. You embody kindness, compassion, and love. You think about the implications of your actions on the whole system, not your little area of interest. Each action you undertake creates a domino effect of positivity or negativity that ripples through your home, company, community, and the world. What would the world look like if all human beings were behaving at their best?

- *Point 7:* At the time of death, my loved ones cannot help me. We die alone, even when we are surrounded by our loved ones. No one can accompany me on that journey. Only the confidence that I have done what life expected from me, letting go of attachment or regrets, will create the inner peace I need to go without resisting the separation from loved ones. Death is a time to let go and forgive. What good does it do to continue carrying a burden? The attachment that I feel to my family, friends, or partners is what causes the greatest fear of death. By knowing that I have been there for them and given them the support, growth, and tools to fulfill their lives, I can go peacefully.

- *Point 8:* At the time of death, my money, status, power, and fame cannot help me. I consider the time I've

spent accumulating. I carry a lot of junk, physically
and figuratively. I may not see myself as a compulsive
shopper, but I participate to some extent in our
consumption economy. The relentless pursuit of wealth,
power, status, and fame may be a satisfying yardstick of
success, but I need to recognize the difference between
needing and wanting. An attachment to these perks,
or a desire for something I do not really need, distorts
my focus and my ability to live the contemplative life
I deserve. More importantly, when the time of death
gets close, I won't take any of these assets with me.
Power and status will be lost, and my money will go to
someone else or the state.

- *Point 9:* At the time of death, my body is of no use.
  I might strive to eat well, exercise, and get enough
  sleep. I might pay attention to the way I look and be
  proud of my appearance. Perhaps I believed that my
  appearance contributed to my success as a leader. Or I've
  taken a contrarian approach and believed that others
  should learn to appreciate me regardless of how I look.
  Either way, appearance is often a topic of attachment
  or aversion. Whichever relationship I have with my
  physical body, I need to be prepared for aging, sickness,
  and death. Eventually, at the time of death, I must let go
  of my body.

The last three points remind us to moderate our attachment to loved ones, material possessions, and physical appearance. It doesn't mean that we should not care. This reflection is about understanding the distinction between caring and attachment, developing the wisdom to let go when we need to.

CONTEMPLATION 4: LEGACY

We all want to know that we mattered. The good news is that you get to be the judge. There is no external standard that you must measure up to or a committee that will review your case and give you an award. You decide what makes up a good life because you always know whether you are giving it your best. The good news is that it is never too late to ask yourself these two questions: "Will I leave the world in a better place than I found it?" and "Did I do my best?"

There is no need to solve climate change or world hunger to leave a legacy. We create a legacy every day through each intentional action and interaction, positive or negative. It is not about the future image of a great accomplishment. Instead, it happens here and now. When you take responsibility and start cleaning your house, figuratively speaking, you create a legacy. You already have all the qualities needed to leave a positive legacy, such as courage, compassion, kindness, loyalty, patience, persistence, or wisdom.

In this contemplation, reflect on the eulogy virtues that you bring to the world or want to develop. Look at the last twenty-four hours. What did you do that makes the world a better place? A worse place? What did you do that did not matter? Repeat the exercise for the last week, month, year, and your life as a whole.

Now, ask yourself: What eulogy virtues would I like to be remembered for? Am I on track? What, if anything, would I do differently tomorrow, even if these are baby steps?

CONTEMPLATION 5: VISUALIZING DEATH

You now have greater clarity about the virtues, responsibility, and positive intentions you want to bring into your everyday life. Now let's move into an even deeper contemplation: visualizing your own death.

Lie down on a bed and imagine that your time has come. Your body has aged and is running out of energy. You feel at peace.

Imagine you have ten breaths left. Bring your awareness to the breath, stable and calm. Start the countdown, enjoying each breath, each one bringing you closer to your death. Ten, nine...eight, seven...continue the countdown until you reach the last three breaths. Three...two...one...Exhale your last breath and relax.

Before you start breathing again, stay there and contemplate the feelings that arise. You are now dead. Life goes on around you. The planet is still at work. Employees commute to the office, children play at recess, families walk in shopping malls.

Life goes on in the wild, too. Animals look for food, birds build nests, cats sleep, dogs bark, insects fly. Winds blows in the forest, rains fall on the plain.

Joy and suffering go on, too. People laugh and cry. Couples make love. Kids play. Patients in hospitals prepare to die. Accidents, wars, oppression, and poverty.

Life goes on, without you. One day, the world will continue without you.

CONTEMPLATION 6:
VISUALIZING DEATH, PART II

This contemplation starts like the previous one. Lie on a bed and count down your last ten breaths as before.

When you are "dead," get up and go out. Imagine that you are now a spirit, invisible and made of pure, loving energy.

Leave your retreat place. Walk around. See how life and the world continues after your death. Just be careful when you cross the streets—no need to hasten the actual time of death.

Finally, reflect and journal on your experience with these last two contemplations. What feelings and realizations came up?

CONTEMPLATION 7: GRATITUDE

This practice was inspired by my friend, Subba. A gratitude practice helps you recognize the blessings in your life and gives meaning to your efforts. It gives you perspective to overcome attachments, selfishness, comparison, jealousy, and narcissism.

As anthropologist and teacher Angeles Arrien writes in *Living in Gratitude*, "Anger, arrogance, and jealousy melt in the embrace of gratitude, and fear and defensiveness dissolve." When we are grateful, we no longer feel isolated and separate but interconnected and part of a shared humanity.

In your journal, make a list of a hundred things for which you are grateful or thankful. Be specific. Do not stop until you have completed the list. Consider your blessings in every dimension—physical, emotional, spiritual, relational, intellectual, and environmental. If you are on a short retreat, list twenty things you are grateful for on every day of your retreat.

When you are done, read the list again, several times. Keep adding to this list every week from now on.

SUMMARY

Rather than ignoring death and burying your head in the sand, you can regard death as your teacher. By embracing the inevitability of death, you start appreciating your finite existence, and you can decide how to best use the time you have, live fully and meaningfully, and reflect on the legacy you want to leave.

In order to familiarize yourself with death, you can practice several contemplations, such as observing death all around you, estimating how much time you have left, creating a sense of urgency through the nine-point Tibetan meditation, reflecting on your legacy, visualizing your own death, and expressing gratitude for your life.

ADDITIONAL JOURNALING
AND REFLECTIONS

- In what did I engage fully today? How am I appreciating every day that I live?
- What is it that I cannot live without?
- What gifts has life bestowed upon me?
- What will remain of my leadership?
- If I die tomorrow, what will I have not accomplished that I want to accomplish?
- If I don't die tomorrow, what would I like to do that would matter?

Chapter 11

EXPANDING WISDOM

L ET'S CONTINUE OUR EXPLORATION OF THE GREAT
human growth themes.

How to define wisdom? Wisdom is a quality we recognize
when we encounter it. Wise leaders exude confidence, equanimity, and inner peace. They have sound judgment and the ability to
simplify even the most complex problems. They show kindness
and compassion toward others. Their acting is wise, but their
being is even wiser.

We express wisdom through our attitude toward the challenges and uncertainties of life. Wise leaders embody calm, curiosity, optimism, and a genuine poise in the face of challenges.

Wisdom is not correlated with intelligence. Many leaders are
smart but foolish. In fact, superior smarts sometimes breed arrogance and contempt.

Wisdom does not come with age, experience, and knowledge. The wise leaders may be old, but old leaders are not always wise.

So, what is wisdom and how can we develop it?

Wisdom involves the ability to see what is, to see the forest for the trees. We carry our ignorance and delusions like a heavy chain. The wise person sees what others don't. This is never more important than in the face of seemingly impossible choices. Intelligence, experience, and knowledge are helpful to identify the options. But only wisdom allows us to decide. When the wise person speaks, the world illuminates. Impossible choices become easy to make.

It could be about a career choice. Should I leave an uninspiring job where going to work every day is a burden? Or should I stay and enjoy financial security and status? Or it could be a management decision. Do I reduce expenses by cutting jobs, or do I protect employment and the livelihood of loyal staff?

RISING ABOVE POLARITIES

We can further define wisdom as the ability to rise above polarities. Polarities are the opposition of two equally powerful alternatives. The benefits of one are the negatives of the other. We are doomed if we choose one and doomed if we choose the other.

Leaders deal with polarities all the time. The more senior they become, the more they must deal with these impossible choices. Easy decisions can be delegated to junior folks. Leaders get to make the calls that no one else wants to make.

God offered young King Solomon anything that his heart might desire. Instead of choosing a long life or the death of his enemies, Solomon requested the ability to distinguish between right and wrong and to be able to govern justly. In return, God gave Solomon not only a wise and discerning mind but also riches and honor.

This story reveals how wealth, success, and fame often come to those who choose to lead wisely. This powerful insight from the Old Testament stands the test of time. There are no short-cuts to wisdom or wealth and success. You must do the time and work. As Carl Jung suggested, we should be wary of unearned wisdom. However, you can create the fertile ground on which the tree of insights, perspective, and understanding will grow.

The perspective-honing component of wisdom can be greatly increased during retreats. Taking time away from noise and clutter allows you to step out of the battlefield and observe it from an external perspective. You can dissociate yourself from the action. You can see what you are doing as an object, not as a subject, once you dissociate from it.

When confronted with complex decisions, leaders can be tempted to ask for more data or more expertise. There is a problem, and we want to solve it by breaking it down into smaller pieces. But as we have seen in Chapter 9, sometimes it is not data, knowledge, or problem-solving that we need. Sometimes, all we need is to let go of our problem-solving mind and shed our fears and anxiety to find a solution. The voice of inner wisdom may be already speaking to us, if only we can hear it.

The shift happens when you realize that it is fear that silences the voice of inner wisdom. Your fear shouts in your head to take the safe alternative. Do what the boss wants or there will be trouble. Make a popular decision so you can be loved. Sit on it and keep options open. Even worse, fear makes you reject your responsibility, such as "I had no choice. They made me do it." This opens the road to every possible unethical behavior, from bad customer service to corporate fraud.

When you let go of your fears, you realize that the polarities are only bogeymen seeking to confuse you. By expanding your view and seeing the system as a whole, you realize that what you perceived as a one-dimensional choice is in fact part of an array of multidimensional possibilities.

A ROADMAP TO WISDOM

Retreats are the perfect setting for listening to your inner voice, keeping your fears in check, and melting polarities away. Away from the noise and clutter, you can see, hear, and feel what matters. Through the previous chapters, we have already progressed a long way toward wisdom. We can appreciate situations in a holistic manner (Chapter 6). We have developed presence and awareness in every moment (Chapter 7). We can give attention and build relationships (Chapter 8). We embrace complexity

(Chapter 9). And we have recognized death as our friend and teacher (Chapter 10).

Now, you can expand on this foundation of wisdom. Let's first take ownership for the results of your actions. Let's look inside and explore your failures and the fears that lead to them. To go deeper, you will work with your own shadow—the dark side of your personality that you are often unconscious of.

Once you have connected to your failures and shadow, you can better contemplate two profound universal laws that are commonly ignored by modern leaders: impermanence and karma. Next, you will be able to approach and defeat polarities. Finally, you will find a reward for doing all this hard work: an immersion in the dark, starry night and the immense depth of the universe.

CONTEMPLATION 1:
OWNING YOUR FAILURES

Life is a constant struggle, and it is that struggle that allows you to grow. Bliss, whenever you achieve it, is an unstable equilibrium. Sooner or later, you will face an obstacle that stops you in your tracks. Along the path, you face disappointments, heartbreaks, professional failures, and loss. There is no growth in success and self-satisfaction. Those who live in their parents' basement because the world is dangerous, those who don't engage in relationships because their heart might be broken, and those who decide to stay within the boundaries they have created for themselves stop growing. It is only by falling a thousand times that a child learns to walk.

You develop by choosing to face a challenge and leaving your comfort zone—even if you fall on your face. There is no certainty of success.

In this first contemplation, list all your failures, personal and professional. Play the movie of your life backwards, starting from today and backtracking. Zoom in on the events that caused you the greatest pain.

For each failure, follow these steps:

1. Ask: What Is Your Responsibility in What Happened?

Failures, like airplane crashes, have many causes, some direct and some with deep roots buried in time. Some result from your decisions, others from your lack of decision. Bad luck happens but this is rarely the only explanation. Failures follow complex patterns.

Earlier, we met Enrique, the once youngest C-Suite member at a global industrial corporation, who felt like an impostor. Recently, Enrique was abruptly fired by his CEO without any warning signs. Enrique felt victimized and enraged. He could not stop speculating about what may have gotten into the deviant mind of the CEO. We turned the table and examined what he could have done wrong. It took us several sessions of reflection to see a pattern of freedom and self-reliance in Enrique's decision-making. Even though he had played the corporate game well and reached the highest level in this large global corporation, he was fundamentally an independent spirit. For a long time, he had silenced the voice in his head that told him to chart his own path. But his attitude showed. The CEO, who demanded full loyalty from his team, may have perceived these signs. Often, by looking for outside causes, we miss the full story.

2. Reflect on the Fears and Ideals that Drive Your Behaviors

Our fears are often repressed or ignored or criticized because they look irrational. Leaders are supposed to be strong. To minimize our spoken or unspoken fears, we pursue an ideal. Fears and ideals drive your behaviors in ways that you cannot understand unless you look inside without hiding from the truth.

The Enneagram is a useful framework to map fears and ideals. It is an ancient system that describes archetypal ego structures. While a description of the Enneagram is beyond our scope, the table on the following page highlights the nine main archetypes and their associated fears and ideals. See which type you can identify with the most.

3. Connect with Your Fears and Ideals, and Value Them with Gratitude

You cannot push them away even if you wanted to. You can only accept them for what they are and recognize that they have played a valuable and protective role, often since childhood. Even if that role is not needed anymore, your only possible course of action is to sincerely show them gratitude.

ENNEAGRAM ARCHETYPE	ROOT FEAR	SELF-IDEAL	POTENTIAL DYSFUNCTIONAL BEHAVIORS
Perfectionist	Fear of being wrong, lazy, corrupt, evil, or defective	I am good, I have integrity	Becoming critical and perfectionistic
Helper	Fear of being unworthy of love or unwanted	I am loved	Becoming possessive, over-caring of others, flattering, people-pleasing, not recognizing your own needs
Achiever	Fear of being worthless and disrespected	I am valuable	Status conscious, overly concerned with image and what others think, overly competitive
Romantic	Fear of meaninglessness	I know my purpose	Becoming moody, disdainful of ordinary ways of life, self-indulgent, and melancholic
Observer	Fear of not knowing, of being incapable	I am capable and competent	Becoming detached yet intense, eccentric, nihilist, and isolated
Loyalist	Fear of chaos	I am safe and supported	Becoming defensive, cautious, indecisive, anxious, and suspicious
Enthusiast	Fear of deprivation and boredom	My needs are fulfilled	Becoming overextended, scattered, undisciplined, distracted, impatient, and impulsive
Challenger	Fear of being controlled or harmed by others	I am in control of my destiny	Becoming egocentric, domineering, confrontational, intimidating, prone to anger, and resisting vulnerability
Peacemaker	Fear of confrontation, separation, or losing harmony	I am at peace	Avoiding conflict and tension, preserving things as they are, resisting change

Chris grew up with an abusive father who not only randomly punished him physically but also ridiculed Chris when he was happy or sad. A Perfectionist, Chris is today a well-adjusted, warm, generous, and friendly senior executive. He realized through our work together that he was struggling to express emotions, having grown up in an environment where he would be punished when he showed sadness or joy. This, in turn, made him want to be competent and righteous and demanding with others. It showed somatically through his great difficulty to feel emotions and sense their impact in his body. This disembodiment made him overly intellectual and superficially rational. Through our work and his own periods of reflection, Chris recognized these patterns, and by connecting with and valuing his protective parts—those that made him afraid of expressing feelings—he progressively unfolded and voiced a much wider range of emotions, in particular with his family and close friends.

The point of this short contemplation is not to replace a coach or therapist. It is to increase awareness of the conditions that have shaped protective patterns. These patterns often emerge in childhood as a protection against being hurt. They remain decades later and drive behaviors. Left unchecked and misunderstood, they contribute to successes and failures. And they always block the full expression of our innate qualities of joy, love, compassion, strength, and stability.

CONTEMPLATION 2: THE SHADOW

Sometimes we struggle with doing what is right. As human beings, we have an innate sense of morality, of good and evil. But our modern culture makes these choices harder.

For thousands of years, religions have guided us. They emerged from the dawn of civilization and captured an essential morality that permeated every aspect of our culture. If we did not know what the right thing to do was, we could always turn to scriptures or a spiritual leader.

In the course of the nineteenth century, the rise of enlightenment and rationalism led to a landmark phenomenon: the disappearance of religion as the beacon of morality. In 1882, philosopher Friedrich Nietzsche saw the danger and famously wrote, in *The Gay Science*:

God is dead. God remains dead. And we have killed him. How shall we comfort ourselves, the murderers of all murderers? What was holiest and mightiest of all that the world has yet owned has bled to death under our knives: who will wipe this blood off us? What water is there for us to clean ourselves? What festivals of atonement, what sacred games shall we have to invent? Is not the greatness of this deed too great for us? Must we ourselves not become gods simply to appear worthy of it?

God was keeping our shadow in check. With the death of God, we saw the rise of ideologies like Marxism, Communism, Maoism, and Nazism. Their leaders played on the collective shadow and gave their populations what they wanted to hear. They led them into mass murder of unprecedented scale.

In our delusion, we often like to believe that if we had lived in that era, we would not have participated in that madness. We would have disobeyed. We would not have spied on our parents and neighbors. We would have resisted. But this is very unlikely. For every ounce of goodness in us, there is a force of darkness of equal proportion. Sometimes, we act out our good qualities, and sometimes our bad ones. The two are always in balance. From our light arises our shadow.

In the warm shelter of the corporation, we do not always choose the path of morality. We will renege on promises. We conspire to eliminate our enemies so we can earn a promotion. We misrepresent facts to win a contract. We bully small suppliers. We practice favoritism and promote our minions instead of more competent individuals. Lobbies misrepresent facts, silence opponents, and splurge on lawmakers to get favorable regulation.

Transgressions are part of everyday corporate life. They reveal the corruption of an entire system, always driven by shadow. We all know companies with deeply toxic cultures. And the list of corporate leaders and politicians who end up in jail keeps getting longer.

Rather than judging and moralizing, you can examine your own actions and motives. It is only by recognizing your own shadow that you create the freedom to choose.

1. Ask Yourself a Set of Questions

What are my own unethical behaviors? Do I lie or misrepresent the truth? Who did I hurt? Am I associated with a company that is irreproachable? Do we, individually or collectively, harm communities or the environment? Do we serve clients who do? Do we buy from companies who do?

We are all, to some extent, part of a system that breaches our own ethical standards. We may bargain that it is not our fault, that we have no choice, or that it would be naïve to believe that this can be avoided.

Take a moment to contemplate the inventory list that you have created. Leave the list open, so you can add to it regularly.

2. Recall Leaders Who Have Transgressed Ethical Boundaries

Perhaps they have committed fraud or tax evasion, caused large-scale environmental destruction, or sold defective products.

You can think of leaders who have been sentenced and sent to jail. Or you can simply consider all the large corporations that legally evade taxes on a massive scale, so their billionaire owners can get richer while not paying taxes to the communities they benefit from.

Now, you may think that you are better, that this would not happen under your watch. Instead, in this contemplation, ask yourself: under what circumstances might I commit these crimes?

We all have our shadow. There is a reason why you notice certain negative behaviors in others. Most likely, these tendencies exist in your shadow. You can either ignore it or establish contact with it. Recognition is half of the solution to preserve the balance.

Take the behaviors that you see in others and that you despise the most. What circumstances could make you be like them?

CONTEMPLATION 3: IMPERMANENCE

We have already discussed impermanence in relationships in Chapter 8, and death in Chapter 10. Let's go deeper by observing how everything changes over time. Like death, impermanence is one of these concepts that we brush aside as self-evident but fail to acknowledge in our actions. We get used to the way things are and seem surprised and pained when they change. Indeed, change and impermanence are major causes of suffering.

You grow your wisdom when you embed the reality of impermanence into your thinking. You may not like change. No one likes to see their lives disrupted by a pandemic, their business threatened by disintermediation, or a favorite subordinate resign. No one wants to lose their loved ones. But when you see the world in constant flux, you realize that change has no intrinsic meaning or quality. It is neither good nor bad. It simply *is*.

Then, consider how everything that you hold as permanent is in fact always changing. Most transformations are not visible to the naked eye. They are too slow. This is the case for changes in nature and climate. This is the case, too, for buildings, cities, roads, and bridges. The house that you occupy today. Mountains, forests, lakes, and deserts. Languages, ideas, religions, laws, states, and currencies.

Now, observe that there is no point clinging to anything. Attachment can only bring suffering. It is best to approach any situation with appreciation and gratitude, and enjoy the present moment. Anything you enjoy or love will eventually disappear. The good news is that any situation you find uncomfortable or unpleasant will also evolve for the better. As the old Persian adage goes, "This, too, shall pass."

Complete this contemplation by taking a walk outdoors. Notice how everything that surrounds you is always in the flow of change. Nothing is permanent.

CONTEMPLATION 4: KARMA

As you sow, so shall you reap. This simple proverb summarizes the law of Karma, or action and reaction. Any intentional action that you complete triggers a chain reaction that will affect you. You can deepen your wisdom by studying Karma, a fundamental pillar of Eastern spiritual traditions such as Hinduism and Buddhism. These traditions teach us a lot, but you do not have to believe in any particular dogma. You can rely on experience and observation to draw your own conclusions.

Karma does not work in mysterious ways. There are two major reasons why Karma works as systematically as the law of gravity. First, your actions have inner consequences. When you yield to the shadow and commit negative actions, you leave a small imprint in your mind. Over time, you become habituated. What you initially considered a transgression becomes routine and you become bolder. The shadow grows in you. The study of criminals is instructive in that respect. No one becomes a criminal overnight. Fraudsters often start with petty theft. Over time, they get emboldened and the magnitude of their transgressions increases. Often, new infractions become necessary to cover up previous ones. To survive, some decide to sail even closer to the wind. The vicious circle continues until they get caught.

Second, your actions have outer consequences. You cannot expect that those you have wronged will not react. The crime may remain unpunished, but it is difficult to sleep at night when you know that at any time, the regulators can show up in your office or the police at your door. A client may realize that you have not fulfilled your contract. Whether you are caught or not, a reputation develops.

When we discuss Karma in retreats, there is always someone who asks why good things happen to bad people. Why does the toxic jerk keep getting promoted? There is no telling how quickly Karma will work, but two things are for sure. First, the jerk has to face their own demons every day. In all honesty, you don't want to exchange your life for theirs even if they get promoted. Second, if many people dislike the jerk already, you are in fact witnessing Karma in action. Observe their reputation, their networks, and ask yourself, is this a pleasant life? You must look beyond the obvious to see how the effects of Karma permeate your psyche, relationships, physical body, and environment.

In this contemplation, take a moment to observe the effects of Karma.

- How did your good actions lead to positive effects?
- How did your bad actions—intentional actions that were committed and completed—have negative consequences across the integral spectrum of your mind, body, relationships, and environment?

CONTEMPLATION 5:
DEALING WITH POLARITIES

Remember that wisdom can be defined as the ability to see beyond polarizations. Simple minds frame the world around them as polarities. Populist politicians, ideologists, and manipulative leaders often say, "You are with me or against me." In their affirmations, they are saying, "All those who belong to this group are good; all others are bad." Statements like these tend to divide and lead to extremes.

Wise leaders refuse to embrace false dichotomies. They can observe that polarities are rarely productive representations of reality. In the face of blunt statements, they always ask: "Is that so?" The truth is never that simple.

We see the world as polarities since our eviction from the womb. Until then, you were one with the other, blessed with warmth, food, and love. Shortly after birth, you started experiencing separation and opposition. Sometimes you are fed (good) or you are hungry (bad). You are comfortable (good) or too cold or too warm (bad). Your mind starts judging in terms of good and bad. For many of us, this tendency remains for the rest of our lives.

We create hierarchies and assign values, so choices become easy. Yoga is better than jogging. Democrats are better than republicans. But a healthy exercise routine can include both the contemplative yoga that brings flexibility, balance, and concentration, and the active jogging that builds our cardiovascular fitness and burns calories. And a healthy society can embody both the rightist qualities of conservatism and conscientiousness and the leftist qualities of open-mindedness and tolerance. Unfortunately, we seem to have lost our ability for wise debate. We prefer to shout our message without listening.

In business, the most difficult decisions arise from polarizations. We are caught between freedom and order. How much should we control and how much should we empower and let go? Should we centralize operations for scale and efficiency, or decentralize for responsiveness and empowerment of the front-liners? Should we organize around product or geographical lines? Should we create individual incentives to encourage strong performers or collective incentives to promote teamwork?

To make their mark, a new leader often changes decisions made by the previous one. Of course, the next leader who comes a few years later reverts those decisions. The pendulum swings endlessly, each generation believing they are right and that those before were idiots. Every new boss wants to bring change. Out with the old, in with the new. "Let's swim together to the magical island where everything will be good." Only the wise realize that the magical island is a mirage that keeps getting further and further away as we swim.

We face polarities across our leadership life: action vs. reflection, horizontality vs. verticality, success vs. conscience, profits vs. sustainability.

Hence, to develop wisdom, we must transcend polarities and escape the either-or mindset. This approach, as counterintuitive as it may seem, is fully embodied in the Taoist concept of Yin and Yang. It invites us to consider that opposites are complementary. We achieve wisdom not by choosing camps but by elevating ourselves to a plane where both camps can coexist. Two sets of opposite ideas can coexist and complement each other. This is not a weak compromise but rather a fusion.

Take a moment to consider an aspect of your leadership where you confront polarities and feel stuck. Two sets of opposite ideas clash with each other. It could be that a group of colleagues wants to pursue a course of action, and another group opposes that view. Or you love your present employer, but the pay is poor. Another firm with a cutthroat reputation has approached you with "an offer you can't refuse."

Polarities arise when benefits and costs are in balance for each option. If the right decision was obvious, you would not be stuck.

Sit comfortably and find a moment of peace. Identify the parts of yourself that are triggered by the situation. In all likelihood, you will identify two parts pulling in opposite directions. Check Chapter 7 to review how to recognize and appreciate the voices that compose your psyche. Perhaps, a part of you is nervous about not earning enough. Another part of you wants you to work in a supportive culture. One by one, establish contact with each part and recognize that each part, in its own ways, wants the best for you. In our example, one part wants you to be financially secure and the other wants you to work in a peaceful environment.

These parts often emerge to protect us from hurt. Deep in your soul, there usually is an original wound. How have you been hurt in the past? Perhaps you grew up with barely enough money for the family to get by. You promised yourself that as an adult, you would never be in this situation again. Or perhaps you hated conflict because it reminded you of your parents fighting. Again, consciously, or not, you decided to seek out harmonious environments.

From the clarity about your original wounds and the parts that protect you today arises a newly found freedom. You are not your parts. Polarizations only emerge when parts pull in different directions. You desire independence but also want fusion with others.

What parts of you are triggered by the polarization you face? How are these parts protecting you from an original wound? Can you value these parts and make them feel seen and understood? If you do, you will feel the release that allows you to transcend the polarization. It is in this release that you will find a space of freedom. Observe the change in your mind, body, and heart.

Let's be clear. Some decisions are hard to make. Yet, we always grow when we connect with the parts that get triggered in a polarizing situation. We can appreciate them. In doing so, you will find new resources inside you that bring us peace and serenity at the time of making difficult choices.

CONTEMPLATION 6: STARGAZING

I would like to finish this chapter on wisdom with a simple contemplation in nature.

In nature, on a clear night, lie down on a comfortable blanket, and look up at the stars. Let go of any intellectualization of your experience. Just be there, with your whole self—mind, heart, and body.

This experience is one that connects you to our shared humanity. It is likely that a thousand generations ago, the tribe from which you descend had the same exact experience in front of the immensity of the universe, the wonders of the stars, and the power of nature.

Most of your subjective experience today, your emotions, your fundamental attachments, fears, and aversions, are the same that your ancestors experienced.

For a moment, as you contemplate the stars, let go of your modern conditioning. Imagine that you are one of the early humans, living in communion with nature. Let that *fundamental wisdom* permeate every cell in your body.

SUMMARY

Wisdom is as much shown in our being as in our actions. It is a quality that is earned, not given, and that shows in the decisions we make and the quality of heart we exhibit. Wisdom emerges in us when we rise above polarities. Polarities divide while wisdom integrates.

To earn your wisdom, you can first look within and reflect on your failures and shadow. You can then contemplate two of the greatest universal laws that are often ignored: impermanence and karma. This equips you to face and rise above polarities. And finally, you can simply observe the universe in awe.

ADDITIONAL JOURNALING
AND REFLECTIONS

- What parts of me do I reject?
- Can I identify inappropriate thoughts?
- Can I acknowledge and accept my repressed shadow? What is the message from my shadow?
- What did I dream about last night? What meaning do I ascribe to the dream?
- What would life be like if I were wise?
- Who are my teachers, mentors, and disciples?

Chapter 12

FINDING PURPOSE

VANESSA EXCELLED AT MEMORIZING AND ANALYZ-
ing. She articulated her thoughts in a logical and compel-
ling manner. So she decided to study law. This was not a choice
born out of passion. Instead, it was a pragmatic decision made
after eliminating less attractive options. Upon graduation, she
joined a reputable law firm. Her hard work, ability to empathize
with clients, and political savviness accelerated her career. She
became a senior partner. While her career blossomed, her personal life stagnated. She dated a few colleagues over the years
but never felt the urge to pause her career to start a family.

Now in her early fifties, earning more than she will ever be
able to spend, Vanessa buys properties around the world but
never has time to visit them. She has lost the fire and ambition she had twenty years ago. She resents the long hours and

incessant client demands. Vanessa longs for a different life, but she doesn't know how to change. She feels trapped in a profession that she once loved but no longer stirs personal growth. She is reluctant to give up her lifestyle of Michelin-star restaurants, first-class travel, and tropical resorts. Sometimes Vanessa wonders about her unlived dreams. She had a passion for animals when she was young. She nearly decided to become a vet, but her dad, a prominent lawyer himself, dissuaded her. For decades, she has donated to animal causes. But she could never adopt a pet given her brutal working hours and travel schedule.

All her friends think that Vanessa has been incredibly successful. Inside, though, she wonders whether she has ever been true to her purpose. What other life could she had lived? As Jungian psychologist Robert Johnson describes it, "In the first half of life, we are busy building careers, finding mates, raising families, fulfilling the cultural tasks demanded of us by society.... But when we reach a turning point at midlife, our psyches begin searching for what is authentic, true, and meaningful."

Many leaders face this conundrum. After many years pursuing a career, they lose the passion that once animated them. They wonder, "Is this what I was meant to do with my life?" Often, they have this uneasy feeling. Despite the outer appearance of success, the pieces of the puzzle do not fit together as well as they used to. Like a priest losing his faith, they start wondering whether they should be doing something else. The veil of illusion is lifting. As philanthropist Bob Buford put it, there comes a point in life when leaders want to graduate from success to significance. They are ready to close a chapter of their life and start a new one.

When the first symptoms of discomfort appear, we rarely know how to read them. You may attribute your uneasiness to outside changes—your job, your company, the market. You explain the feeling away: "It's normal, after so many years, to want something different." Or "Perhaps I need a vacation." It may take a long time to realize that the questioning is not going away.

The forces of homeostasis are often greater than our willingness or ability to look inside. You are busy with little time to listen to your soul. There is always something more important to do: closing a deal, earning a promotion, choosing a vacation destination. You bargain with yourself and buy a few more years. Life is not so bad after all. Why rock the boat? When the discomfort comes, it is easy to numb it with a nice beach vacation or a new car.

To make matters worse, you don't know where to turn to for guidance. Those closest to us don't understand us, with comments such as "You're having a midlife crisis. It will pass." or, "Don't be stupid. Look at all you've achieved. What are you complaining about?"

To find purpose, you must first awaken. It be may sudden or progressive. Carl Jung said, "Your vision will become clear only when you can look into your own heart. Who looks outside, dreams; who looks inside, awakes." It may take years before you find the courage to face the inevitable inquiry into your purpose.

THE ROAD LESS TRAVELED

External events may be the cause of your awakening. Deep personal loss opens our minds and plunge us into a reflective mood.

It can be a career accident. One day, you are on top of the world. The next, you get fired and your world crashes. Past the initial shock, some decide to get back on the saddle and start riding another horse immediately. Others want to find answers and realize that the accident may be a blessing in disguise.

Sometimes, the loss of a loved one or a health scare may also be a wake-up call. It is often the realization of our own mortality that prompts us to use the rest of our time meaningfully.

Sometimes, you grow out of the choices that you made or were made for you in your twenties. You have satisfied your need for career success. You have possessions and ego gratification. You now find that the exciting path you followed so far has lost its appeal. You reach a fork in the road. On the left is a well-lit highway. It is safe and familiar. But like a mirage, the destination that once appeared so clearly on the horizon doesn't seem to be any closer. The reward for traveling a thousand miles on that road is that you earn the right to travel another thousand miles.

The road on the right is unknown. There are no markings, and it doesn't show on your GPS. It is intriguing, but you are afraid, too. What if you lost everything you have worked so hard for?

Like Vanessa, many of the clients I work with have reached that fork in the road. To help them, I invite them to look within and reflect on their motivations.

The quest for purpose is not about achieving fame, wealth, a beautiful body, or success. It is not about finding an easier way to make a living. It is the realization that after achieving what you desired, you still long for a sense of satisfaction. You have outgrown your cravings for external stimulation and validation. You can now proceed toward your quest for transcendence.

For some, this awakening comes with the painful realization that they followed the wrong tracks all along. They climbed the ladder to the top only to realize it was leaning against the wrong wall. I often caution clients not to throw the baby out with the bathwater. It is because you have lived through your first half of life that you can now decide what you want for the second half. You have achieved competence, credibility, and the financial freedom that allows you to pursue a new quest.

You can only hope that this awakening happens in your life-time. In his collection of essays titled *Consolations*, Anglo-Irish poet David Whyte captures the vacuity of ambition beautifully: "Ambition is natural to the first steps of youth who must experience its essential falsity to know the larger reality that stands behind it, but held onto too long, and especially in eldership, it always comes to lack surprise, turns the last years of the ambitious into a second childhood, and makes the once successful into an object of pity."

This realization calls for a reassessment of your life. You may perceive that, like a butterfly strives to break free from its cocoon, a new sense of direction is struggling to emerge. You need to respond to the call. This is no longer about what you want from life but what life expects from you. Whether riches await at the end of your Camino is irrelevant when you make the decision to start walking. The journey is the destination.

But how do you know that you are not chasing a mirage, that you are not infatuated with some romantic idea of purpose?

TURNING INWARD

Finding purpose requires a shift from external sources of satisfaction—material goods, sense pleasures, popularity, and status—toward internal ones. The Greek philosophers first noticed that their elites loved indulging in pleasures that stimulate the senses, such as work, food, sex, partying, or sports. They called this quest for pleasure *hedonia*. Our modern culture has made hedonia the ultimate holy grail. The rich and famous are a permanent display of hedonia. They have their mansions, cocktail dresses, exotic vacations, luxury meals, and private jets. In Los Angeles, London, Dubai, or Shanghai, the model of successful life is similar.

But the Greeks knew that hedonia can only provide superficial and temporary satisfaction. Consumption never provides lasting fulfillment. One day, we will wake up and wonder what we have been doing all these years. Imagine your obituary saying, "They spent their life pursuing pleasurable experiences."

To balance hedonia, the philosophers identified the importance of *eudaimonia*, the quest for human flourishing and virtue. You start on the path of eudaimonia through the combination of contemplation and purposeful action. When you still the senses and find calm and serenity, you see how you can contribute to yourself and others. This is not about short-term arousal of the senses but delayed gratification. You know that your efforts today will bear fruit tomorrow. You find eudaimonia in the pursuit of activities that makes you grow. It could be learning, loving, teaching, building, or contributing to a cause greater than yourself. You grow and help others grow. Eudaimonia is born out of presence and engagement.

This is challenging in a culture that encourages narcissism and staging ourselves on social media. But the quest for purpose requires you to seek and practice authenticity and humility. Contemplative leaders are a voice of reason and wisdom when others are seeking pleasure and self-promotion.

You do not need to save the world to find meaning in daily life. You can find a way to support your staff. You engage with your suppliers and go beyond the call of duty with customers. You bring calm and clarity in the midst of heated and adversarial negotiations. You respond with presence to anyone who reaches out for help. You find ways to impact others positively and create a halo of inspiration and kindness.

THE FRUITS OF LABOR

In the *Bhagavad Gita*, Lord Krishna admonishes Prince Arjuna: "You have a right to perform your prescribed duty, but you are not entitled to the fruits of action. Never consider yourself to be the cause of the results of your activities, and never be attached to not doing your duty." Arjuna, a leader, has come to the battlefield to fight and win. Krishna reminds him that you should perform your actions for their own sake and never with an extrinsic end in mind.

The ideal described by Krishna is clear: your work is your practice, and your career is a lifetime of practice. When you are at your best, you work not for self-glorification but because it is the expression of the meaning you give to your life. When you are more interested in results and rewards than in the work itself, you have not found your purpose despite what you may believe. You still crave hedonia.

Viktor Frankl was an Austrian psychiatrist who spent several years in a Nazi concentration camp. He reflected on what gives meaning to life. He noticed that some prisoners took responsibility and determined not to let themselves be the victims. They tended to survive. But those who were defeated by the circumstances tended not to. Based on his observations, Frankl believed we should not pursue happiness but instead seek joy and meaning in everything we do.

Reflecting on his experience, Frankl wrote, "Man's search for meaning is the primary motivation in his life and not a 'secondary rationalization' of instinctual drives. This meaning is unique and specific in that it must and can be fulfilled by him alone; only then does it achieve a significance that will satisfy his own will to meaning."

The stakes are high. Several research studies have shown that adults who have a strong purpose in life live longer. Purpose makes us more resilient to the difficulties that we encounter in our leadership. Frankl also wrote, "Once an individual's search for meaning is successful, it not only renders him happy but also gives him the capability to cope with suffering."

Ultimately, finding purpose only requires satisfying a few criteria. You must love the work you are doing, not only for the enjoyment it provides (hedonia) but also for the meaning and sense of fulfillment that you attach to it (eudaimonia). This is a subjective choice that requires coherence with your values. You must be clear what those are in the first place.

THE VOICE OF YOUR SOUL

You cannot hear the voice of your soul in a noisy world. It is too easy to mistake the forest for the trees when you believe the fairy tales on social media. Or you struggle with impossible comparisons to the rich and famous. Retreats and contemplation provide you with the necessary silence to hear your inner guide.

Author and educator Parker Palmer wrote in *Let Your Life Speak*, "From the beginning, our lives lay down clues to selfhood and vocation, though the clues may be hard to decode. But trying to interpret them is profoundly worthwhile—especially when we are in our twenties or thirties or forties, feeling profoundly lost, having wandered, or been dragged, far away from our birth right gifts."

According to Palmer, "Vocation does not come from a voice 'out there' calling me to become something I am not. It comes from a voice 'in here' calling me to be the person I was born to be, to fulfill the original selfhood given me at birth by God."

In my experience, the call does not come in a flash of sudden realization. Instead, you need to take your time, observe how your life has unfolded, and learn the lessons. When did you last feel energized and purposeful? What did you love doing as a child? Who inspires you? What articles or books make you dream? The answers are here, waiting for you to discover them.

For some, finding purpose will mean reinventing your life. Psychology magazines and self-help books are full of stories of investment bankers teaching yoga, management consultants starting an organic farm, and marketing managers becoming nuns.

But for many, the change will not be so drastic. Sometimes, you need to simply apply a fresh coat of paint and open the windows to let the breeze in. You may stay with the same firm but in a different role. In my own transformation, I continued serving the financial institutions that were my clients at McKinsey. But instead of offering them strategic advice and restructuring plans, I started helping them with their leadership teams. Over time, the metamorphosis continued as my interests, practice, and client base shifted.

Here are a few contemplations you can use during a retreat focused on purpose. Each one will help you hear the call of your soul.

CONTEMPLATION 1: LIFE JOURNEY

The journey to purpose starts with taking stock. For this contemplation, you will need blank sheets of paper, pens, and color highlighters. Drawing your journey allows you to observe the patterns that govern your life, for they often are the imprints of your soul. Day after day, your soul speaks to you. For example, certain activities, places, individuals, situations, and atmospheres attract you. Yet, you do not always know how to listen.

The answer is always with you. In the interstices of your life, you sometimes manage to notice the true calling. It is when we are not busy and on autopilot that life expresses itself. You notice what truly fills you with joy, energy, and passion.

When I look back at my own story, I can see how I was always drawn to the field of personal development and spirituality. In my early twenties, I wanted a successful business career.

I grew up in a middle-class family, and financial rewards were my measure of success. This led me to the world of finance. But I was also reading about psychology, body work, mysticism, and yoga. It took me thirty years to find a way to integrate all these dimensions into my current advisory and retreat practice. I often wonder what would have happened if I had been able to read the signs earlier. What if I had listened to my desire to understand the mysteries of the human soul? This is the paradox of purpose. It is only after chasing success that you can realize it was never the only answer.

I loved my work at McKinsey and kept quiet about my "other" interests. One day, I knew I had found my calling. One of our partners in Australia was doing transformative work with clients. He had enlisted the help of spiritual coaches and neuroscience experts. This resonated with me in a profound way. For the first time, I realized that it was possible to bring the contemplative disciplines to teams of senior executives without being called a charlatan. This was a major turning point in my life. I left McKinsey and the world of financial services a few years later to pursue work with leadership teams. I went into executive search. To find more freedom and escape politics, I started my own firm. It took me another several years to develop and shape my contemplative leadership approach. What is fascinating about the following life journey exercise is that it shows how all the signs are always here if you only care to listen.

Step 1: Drawing My Life Journey

- Take one or several sheets of paper and let your imagination do the drawing. Draw a line representing your life. Segment your life into its most important chapters.

- Describe each chapter briefly. What were your thoughts, hopes, and fears during that time? Who were the important people who influenced you, whether positively or negatively? What were you doing? What environment—at home or work—were you in?

- Now, identify the high and low points during each chapter of your life journey. A high point is when you felt energized, on the top of the world. A low point is when you were beaten and defeated or when your life broke down. You can highlight the highs in green and the lows in red. What created the high points? What provoked the low points?

- Next, examine the transitions to the next chapter. What provoked the end of one chapter and the beginning of the next? Was the transition voluntary? Was it positive? You can highlight the key decisions or critical factors that triggered a transition in yellow.

- Lastly, examine the important decisions you made and highlight them in yellow, too. What fork in the road did you arrive at? What path did you take? What path did you not take?

Step 2: Review and Reflection

- Review your lifeline. Give a title to each chapter. What is the chapter's main message or lesson? What is the chapter teaching you about yourself and the world? What stories were you telling yourself at the time? Are these stories still true?

- What patterns can you observe from your high and low points? From your decisions? From the roads taken and not taken?

- As writer Po Bronson points out, curiosity is a raw and genuine sign from deep inside our tangled psyches, and we'd do well to follow the direction it points us. What have you been consistently curious about?

- What are the key events that have made you who you are today?

- What strengths and qualities did you exhibit? How do these qualities manifest themselves chapter after chapter?

- What indications does each chapter give you about your life's purpose? Now that you are listening, what is their call?

CONTEMPLATION 2: VALUES

It has become fashionable for businesses to proclaim their values. These are usually a variation of boilerplate themes such as integrity, innovation, leadership, collaboration, diversity, courage, excellence, respect, care for others, or inspiration. They look great on a company's website. The real test, of course, is how the leaders live these values in complex situations. Particularly, what happens when the bottom line is at risk?

As leaders, we must be clear about our own values before adopting a blanket statement produced by a communication agency. What are the principles that inspire your vision and guide your decisions? Your values only reveal themselves when they are tested. When the sailing is smooth, you can proclaim anything. When the weather gets rough, you must make choices. Carry on the journey, at the risk of losing your life, or return to port and give up on the quest? It is when your personal safety is at risk that you know whether your values hold.

Joan Chittister, an American Benedictine nun and theologian, wrote, "The great leaders of history have always been those who refused to barter their ideals for the sake of their personal interests and who rebelled against the lies of their times. Real leaders don't live to get to the top of a system. They live to save the soul of it."

You can contemplate the following questions to clarify your values:

- Make an initial list of the values that seem important. To help, you can recall situations of peak experience, when you felt that your professional life was flowing. What values were expressed? You can also recall situations when you were uncomfortable, angry, or frustrated. How did the situation conflict with your values?

- As a leader, have you been in situations where your values conflicted with others? How did you resolve the outer conflict? What did you learn about yourself?

- Have you been in situations where you made decisions that conflicted with your values? How did you resolve the conflict within? What did you learn about yourself?

CONTEMPLATION 3:
INNER AND OUTER IMPACT

As a leader, what significance do you want to give to your action and what impact do you want to have on the world? You have unique qualities—the power to create a vision, to chart a course, to influence others, to inspire action, to execute well. You must accept that it is also your responsibility to direct these qualities toward a goal that is meaningful to you.

In Chapter 6, we reviewed the differences between intrinsic and extrinsic motivators. Your leadership journey is determined by the impact you want to have on the world. Take a couple of hours to reflect on the following questions:

- How do your values drive the work you should be doing?

- What work can satisfy both your intrinsic and extrinsic motivational needs?

- What is your gift to the world? What are the key strengths—such as experience; skills; networks; leadership capabilities; character traits; or cognitive, emotional, physical, or spiritual intelligence—you bring to the world?

- What impact do you see yourself having on your colleagues, clients, family, and community?

- How much passion do you bring to your work? Would others describe you as a passionate leader? Do you find passions outside of work? How do you integrate both worlds?

- Do you derive joy or meaning from your relationships at work? Are you bringing joy and meaning to others? Do you work with friends, people whom you enjoy meeting outside work and with whom you share common interests? Why or why not?

- Do you feel that you belong to one or several communities, at work and outside of work? Are you leading a community? Are you a significant contributor to a community? Do you gain meaning from the communities to which you belong? Why or why not?

- Are you in touch with your feelings and emotions at work? Do you know how certain activities and situations affect your mood? Can you influence these? Why or why not? What do you do to be at your best when you lead?

- Do you feel that you are generally in control of your environment? Aside from the inevitable emergencies and unexpected setbacks, do you get a sense that life is flowing? Or is life a succession of emergencies and disasters that require your attention, with days never ending the way you expected? How can you return to a sense of flow and serenity?

CONTEMPLATION 4: THE HERO JOURNEY

Since the dawn of civilization, the adventures of heroes have inspired us. Heroes leave the comfort of their homes to pursue a perilous mission against powerful enemies. They triumph and return home with wealth and wisdom. These stories have been told around the campfire and transmitted over thousands of generations. My favorite hero journey is that of Frodo in Tolkien's *Lord of the Rings*.

The archetype of the hero is one of the most powerful in our collective human psyche. It never fails to inspire awe, admiration, and respect, among young and old alike.

The late Joseph Campbell was a professor of literature specializing in comparative mythology. He studied epic tales and traditional myths across civilizations. He found that those stories, many of which are thousands of years old, follow a similar pattern. Namely, he found that we all have a quest in life. Fulfilling that quest is dangerous and many refuse the call, daunted by the perilous journey in front of them and the elusiveness of the reward.

True leaders are those who heed the call and pursue a cause greater than themselves. They do not pursue power, riches, and fame for their own sake. Instead, every day, they accept the challenges and battles that present themselves in pursuit of their quest. They believe that the forces of good must triumph and that they can make the world a better place.

True leaders can be afraid, too. The difference between them and ordinary people is not in the confidence that they will succeed. It is in embarking on a journey that offers no guarantee of positive outcomes. There is only the satisfaction, day in and day out, of walking the path for its intrinsic rewards.

As Campbell put it: "A hero ventures forth from the world of common day into a region of supernatural wonder; fabulous forces are there encountered and a decisive victory is won; the hero comes back from this mysterious adventure with the power to bestow boons on his fellow man."

Campbell demonstrated that all hero journeys follow a similar sequence, which I have simplified here:

- *Step 1:* We are in the known, ordinary world. We live peacefully, and life is good. We could continue like this forever. However, dark clouds are gathering on the horizon.

- *Step 2:* The peace of the ordinary world is threatened. The forces of evil are manifesting themselves more strongly every day.

- *Step 3:* At first, we may be reluctant to accept the call for action, until we realize that our world is at risk. We do not want to step into the unknown. Gradually, we develop the conviction, often with great doubts, that we must heed the call.

- *Step 4:* We assemble a fellowship, a group of intrepid and trusted companions, to travel with us. Often, we receive the help of a wise, old mentor. We cross the point of no return. This commitment is an exhilarating, yet unsettling peak experience.

- *Step 5:* We step into the unknown and begin our travels. Our strength and leadership are tested daily, as we fight battle after battle. We build new relationships, we encounter new allies, we are shocked to discover that some of our friends are traitors, and we realize that our enemies are even stronger than we imagined. At one point, we are nearly defeated. We feel hopeless, and we wonder if quitting would be the right choice. But quitting means the death of our ideals.

- *Step 6:* Eventually, we overcome adversity. We rescue the princess, slay the dragon, or find the gold. The forces of evil are defeated.

- *Step 7:* We can now return home, where the journey started. It is only then that we realize how much we have changed. The experience has transformed us profoundly, and we will never again be the same person. We are scarred. We have witnessed ugliness, deceit, and evil in proportions that we could not have fathomed. But we have also been blessed with beauty, truth, and goodness that those living in the ordinary world cannot appreciate. We needed to embark on the quest to discover a new, deeper wisdom.

To close this retreat and this book, I invite you to reflect on your own hero journey.

- Familiarize yourself with the steps of the hero journey described above, by recalling your own favorite hero stories.
- What is your quest?
- What has prepared you for the journey?
- What is the call? Why must you heed the call? What makes it so powerful?
- How does the call align with your values (those identified during Contemplation 3)?
- Could someone else take the quest and fight the monsters? Do you have to do it yourself?
- Who is the guide, the mentor, the person who will provide encouragement and wisdom on your quest?
- What is the first battle you must fight? Or have you already fought a battle and realized that maybe you could live to tell the tale?
- For how long have you been on this quest? Are you at the beginning, on your way, or nearing triumph and the return home?

- What monsters must you fight? What scares you the most? Is there any chance, if you refuse to embark, that the monsters will go away?
- What is the reward of your quest?
- What are your secret weapons and superpowers?
- Will you be traveling alone, or is there a group of courageous warriors to accompany you? How will you convince them that they should join you?
- How does putting your journey in this perspective influence the way you lead?
- What have you learned about yourself so far on this journey?

SUMMARY

Ultimately, you complete your integration when you confront your quest for purpose. Without purpose, you are just "killing time" or mindlessly seeking elusive extrinsic pleasures. With purpose, your life finds meaning.

You will not find the answers about your purpose outside yourself. They can only be found within and have been here all along, if only you can listen to the voice of your soul. For this, you can first look for clues in your life journey. Then, you can reflect on your values and the impact you want to have. Lastly, you can reflect metaphorically on your very own "hero journey" that allows you to find personal growth at work and in life.

ADDITIONAL JOURNALING
AND REFLECTIONS

Your answers to the following questions will offer clues to what speaks to your soul:

- Who and what do I admire?
- What heroes inspire me?
- What makes me a better person?
- What am I committed to?
- What did I love doing when I was ten or fifteen years old?
- If I listened attentively to the voice of my soul, what would I hear?
- When was the last time I was totally and effortlessly absorbed in an activity?
- What was the last book or article that captivated me? What places, people, and activities am I drawn to?
- If I had one extra month this year, with no obligations and constraints whatsoever, what would I do?

CONCLUSION

You become a contemplative leader once you stop seeking answers outside yourself. At this point, you no longer hold the traditional view that the present is imperfect. You no longer believe that only change can bring salvation. There is no magical island. You have finally transcended the myth of self-improvement and the need to correct your so-called deficiencies.

You can meet your desire to grow with a kind and generous approach. You know you are whole already and have everything you need to be successful. The question is no longer: How can I fix myself or my business? It becomes: How can I access the inner resources that are always present in me? How can I unleash these qualities so they can manifest and flow freely?

All along, the answers were within you. They always have been. You had lost sight of this fundamental truth, busy as you were chasing your tail. This is the great paradox of our times. In an era of extreme individualism and self-display, we rarely take time to look within. You know what you want to look like externally, but you don't know who you are inside. Rather than feeling whole, you feel overwhelmed or deficient.

We have traveled together and explored how to break this vicious circle by creating a space of reflection and exploration. A retreat is nothing but a gateway to reconnect with yourself. It provides the space to find clarity, balance, and purpose. These three elements are the precondition for your leadership to unfold. Only then can you simultaneously accomplish what you are meant to do and become who you are meant to be.

We can hold retreats anywhere, from a coffee shop to a monastery, from a hotel room to a cabin by the lake. Retreats can be as short as two hours wedged between meetings or extend over several days or weeks. We must claim our right to retreat.

YOUR JOURNEY

The journey of Being is ongoing. Return to the chapters whenever you need to reset. The first five chapters (Part 1) covered what you need to get started. They highlight the challenges facing modern leaders (Chapter 1) and the benefits of retreats (Chapter 2). We defined a retreat (Chapter 3), how to design one (Chapter 4), and how to take the first baby steps (Chapter 5).

The seven themes in Part 11 provided a simple yet powerful roadmap to connect with yourself. Chapter 6 exposed the tools needed to contemplate a journey, such as taking stock and using an integral map. Chapter 7 was about showing up in the world. To be present, you must deepen your self-awareness. Chapter 8 applied the teachings of Chapter 7 to the area of relationships. You learned to appreciate your interconnectedness and deepen your understanding of others. Chapter 9 dealt with complexity. Instead of ignoring or denying it, you learned to embrace and dance with it. Chapter 10 approached death as our ultimate teacher. You do not have to like the idea of death, but you cannot ignore it anymore. With these critical insights assimilated, Chapter 11 explored wisdom as a leader's ability to end polarization. Finally, Chapter 12 offered guidance to reflect on purpose. It asks not what you expect from life but what life expects from you.

THE ROAD AHEAD

Your journey does not stop here. This is only the beginning. Now that we have walked the first mile together, you can continue unfolding on your own. You have all the tools you need.

The connection you have established with yourself is always available, always accessible, here and now. Remember the Four Ss framework and curate your own retreats. Settle down in a conducive *space*, find refuge in *solitude* and *silence*, and be open to connecting with your *spirit*. Don't wait to organize your first retreat if you have not done so yet!

I am grateful to be a small part of your unfolding as a leader. Now, I hope you continue shining your bright light on the world. By reading this book and curating your own retreats, you will be even more of a force for good. The world needs you.

In the appendix, you will find a list of books that you can bring on retreats to continue exploring and further your contemplative journey.

If you have found this book helpful in guiding you along the path of contemplative leadership, I would love to hear from you. You can contact me at *fabrice@desmarescaux.com*.

BOOKS AND ARTICLES
TO BRING ON RETREATS

CHAPTER 6: MAPPING THE JOURNEY

*A Theory of Everything: An Integral Vision for Business, Politics, Science,
and Spirituality*, by Ken Wilber

*Authentic Happiness: Using the New Positive Psychology to Realize Your
Potential for Lasting Fulfillment*, by Martin Seligman

The Power of Habits: Why We Do What We Do in Life and Business, by
Charles Duhigg

CHAPTER 7: CULTIVATING PRESENCE

Good Work: Meditation for Personal & Organizational Transformation,
by Laurence Freeman

How Emotions Are Made: The Secret Life of the Brain, by Lisa Feldman
Barrett

Search Inside Yourself: The Unexpected Path to Achieving Success, Happiness (and World Peace), by Chade-Meng Tan

CHAPTER 8: DEEPENING RELATIONSHIPS

Difficult Conversations: How to Discuss What Matters Most, by Douglas Stone, Bruce Patton, Sheila Heen

"How Will You Measure Your Life?", article by Clayton Christensen (*Harvard Business Review*, July-August 2010)

Nonviolent Communication: A Language of Life, by Marshall B. Rosenberg

Time to Think: Listening to Ignite the Human Mind, by Nancy Kline

CHAPTER 9: DANCING WITH COMPLEXITY

"A Leader's Framework for Decision Making", article by David Snowden, Mary Boone (*Harvard Business Review*, November 2007)

Essential Spirituality: The 7 Central Practices to Awaken Heart and Mind, by Roger Walsh

In Over Our Heads: The Mental Demands of Modern Life, by Robert Kegan

Thinking, Fast and Slow, by Daniel Kahneman

CHAPTER 10: EMBRACING DEATH

A Year to Live: How to Live This Year as If It Were Your Last, by Stephen Levine

Living in Gratitude: A Journey That Will Change Your Life, by Angeles Arrien

Mind of Clear Light: Advice on Living Well and Dying Consciously, by Dalai Lama XIV

The Death of Ivan Ilyich, by Leo Tolstoy
The Five Invitations: Discovering What Death Can Teach Us About Living Fully, by Frank Ostaseski

CHAPTER 11: EXPANDING WISDOM

A New Earth: Awakening to Your Life's Purpose, by Eckhart Tolle
Ageless Soul: An Uplifting Meditation on the Art of Growing Older, by Thomas Moore
Essence of the Bhagavad Gita: A Contemporary Guide to Yoga, Meditation, and Indian Philosophy, by Eknath Easwaran
Wild: From Lost to Found on the Pacific Crest Trail, by Cheryl Strayed
The Wisdom of the Enneagram: The Complete Guide to Psychological and Spiritual Growth for the Nine Personality Types, by Don Richard Riso, Russ Hudson

CHAPTER 12: FINDING PURPOSE

Let Your Life Speak: Listening for the Voice of Vocation, by Parker Palmer
Living Your Unlived Life: Coping with Unrealized Dreams and Fulfilling Your Purpose in the Second Half of Life, by Robert Johnson, Jerry Ruhl
Man's Search for Meaning, by Viktor E. Frankl
Transitions, by William Bridges
Working Identity: Unconventional Strategies for Reinventing Your Career, by Herminia Ibarra

ACKNOWLEDGMENTS

I would like to thank:

My executive coaching and retreat buddies: Gregoire Amigues, Benoit Auger, Rob Bier, Pierre Fel, San Lai, Cathrin Lindenau, and Thierry de Panafieu.

My mentors and teachers on this path toward clarity, balance, and purpose: Zafer Achi, Vajiro Chia, Laurence Freeman OSB, Ken Gibson, Mark Hansen, Etienne Jaugey, Cathy Johnson, Stuart Ludwig, Steve March, and Lama Zopa Rinpoche.

The seekers who shared their retreat experience with me: Janet Drey, Emma, Mayank Parekh, Stéphane Targui, and Subba Vaidyanathan.

My clients over the last twenty years. You know who you are. Your trust in me means everything. I have learned so much from you all.

Ilian Mihov, James Shaheen, Loren Shuster, and Oliver Tonby for their kind endorsements.

The great team at Scribe Media and in particular Annaliese Hoehling, Chas Hoppe, Simon Kerr, John Mannion, Erik van Mechelen, Erin Michelle Sky, Lauren Smith, and Neddie Ann Underwood.

Jocelyne Lee Dubos for her wonderful illustrations.

The many colleagues who put up with my experiments, including Chan Wai Leong, Raoul Nacke, and Dimitri Tsamados.

And Shan, for allowing me to follow my path and supporting me in more ways than I thought possible.

Thank you all from the heart.